Brownie Guide Handbook

Written by Lynda Neilands

Edited by Vronwyn Thompson, Caroline Arthur and Kathryn Cleary

Designed by Joanne Harkness

Illustrated by Jan Lewis, Teresa Foster and Lucy Su

THE GUIDE
ASSOCIATION

Acknowledgements

The *Brownie Guide Handbook* Working Group:
Kate Harding, Susan Jones, Marian Mole, Karen Rogers, Jackie
Shoebridge, Shirley Torrens

The Challenges were devised by a group of Brownie Guiders
representing each Country/Region of the United Kingdom.

Published by The Guide Association
17 – 19 Buckingham Palace Road
London SW1W 0PT

New Edition 1995
© The Guide Association 1995

ISBN 0 85260 127 1

Paper supplied by Precision Publishing Papers Ltd, Yeovil
Origination by Positive Colour Ltd, Maldon, Essex
Printed in England by Butler & Tanner Ltd, Frome

The text paper is Dorchester Text 110 gsm. The eucalyptus tree, which forms the major constituent, is a fast maturing, high yielding and environmentally friendly crop. The paper is elemental chlorine free.

Guiders are reminded that during the lifespan of this publication, policy changes may be made by The Guide Association which will affect the accuracy of information contained within these pages.

It's Emily's Birthday

'Great! I'm seven! I can be a Brownie now.'

'Please can I go to Brownies, Mum?' she asks her mother at breakfast.

'I know you're on the waiting list. I'll telephone Mrs James and ask her,' her mum replies.

Mrs James says she would love to have Emily in the Pack.

And so, on Friday afternoon, Mrs Martin takes Emily to the Brownie hall and waves goodbye.

Inside, everyone looks very busy! It's a bit scary – but Mrs James soon helps Emily feel at home.

A girl called Sarah chooses Emily for her partner.

Why are you wearing that?

It's my tabard. It's what I wore at Rainbows.

Sarah is a new Brownie, too. Before coming to Brownies she was a Rainbow.

Emily asks Sarah what Rainbows was like. 'It was great,' Sarah tells her. 'We tried all sorts of things I hadn't done before. I liked making masks best.'

These are the words Sarah said as a Rainbow: 'I will do my best to love my God and to be kind and helpful.'

Soon Sarah will promise to do her best as a Brownie. 'I'll be a real Brownie then,' she tells Emily, 'and I'm going to have a yellow sweatshirt, instead of my tabard.'

The first few weeks are so exciting. Emily learns a lot about being a Brownie. It's such fun, she can hardly wait for Friday afternoons. She joins in all the games and activities.

She is one of the friendliest Brownies in the Pack, which is why we've asked her to be your friend and to help you, right from the beginning.

'There's so much to tell you about Brownies. I'll start with Brownie Sixes. This is my Six.'

This is my Six.

Sue

Jill

Helen

Linda

Karen

'Sixes work together at meetings. Here we are acting out a nursery rhyme for the rest of the

Baaa!

Baaa!

Baaa!

Baaa!

'Brownie Packs are made up of Sixes, each with a different name. My Six is called the Pixies. Linda is the leader (called the Sixer) and Karen is the Second. Karen helps Linda to run the Six. Sometimes when I don't understand something I ask Linda to explain.'

'Is your Six one of these, or has your Pack chosen a different name?'

'There's a page for writing about your Six in your *Brownie Promise Book.*'

The Brownie Guide Song

Brownies have their own very special song.

We're Brown-ie Guides, we're Brown-ie Guides, we're here to lend a hand.___ To love our God and serve our Queen and help our homes and land.___ We've Brown-ie friends, we've Brown-ie friends in North, South, East and West,___ We're joined to-ge-ther in our wish to try to do our best.

The Brownie Guide Ring

'The Guiders make a gate. We skip through in our Sixes singing the Brownie Song to "lah" and clapping.

'We make a circle around the toadstool while we sing the song.

'Then it is time for notices. Mrs James reminds us of dates and times of any special events. She may also collect our subscriptions (the money we bring so that she can pay for all the different things the Pack needs).

'You can make your circle round a Brownie flag, a pool or a large World Badge, but you will make it in the same way as we do, and you'll sing the same song. Sometimes, before leaving the Ring, we all hold hands and sing the song again.'

This is the way we make a Brownie Ring.

Brownie Bells

O Lord our God, Thy child-ren call,

Grant us Thy peace, And bless us all

At the end of our meeting, we sing a prayer called Brownie Bells and then we all go home.

The Brownie Guide Sign

'Brownie Guides, Guides, Ranger Guides, Young Leaders, Guiders and Commissioners all make the sign in this way. It shows that we all belong to the same Guide family and have made a Promise with three parts. (Three parts – three fingers.)'

We're all part of a family.

'Bring your right hand up to your shoulder, palm facing forwards, fingers straight. Now hold your little finger down with your thumb. That's it!'

'Making the sign with your right hand means using your left hand to shake hands – unless you've got a spare hand!'

The Brownie Guide Motto

'"I've only got one pair of hands!" Mum used to say when the telephone rang and Sophie cried and Nipper wanted to go out at the same time.'

Waa-Waaaa!

'She can't say *that* now because I'm a Brownie. The Brownie Guide Motto is "Lend a Hand" (L.A.H. for short), so now Mum has a second pair of hands in the house . . . MINE!'

14

'These are my Lend a Hand pictures for last week. (Jill helped me draw them.) As you can see it isn't only Mum who needs a hand. Teachers and neighbours and all sorts of other people do too.'

'A motto is a saying to live by. So wherever you are, remember our Motto and be ready to carry it out. There's a page for your L.A.H. drawings in your *Brownie Promise Book*.'

The Pack Salute

'Here we are welcoming a Brownie who has just made her Promise. We are giving her a Pack Salute.

'We clap three times, once above our heads, once to the right and once to the left. With each clap we call "Welcome". Then we stand still and make the Brownie Guide sign, and our new member makes the sign back.'

'Sometimes, we can use different words. When Sue's dad showed us a film on road safety, we said "Thank you", instead of "Welcome", each time we clapped.'

'And when Jill won first prize in a colouring competition we said "Well done".'

BROWNIE Magazine

'One Friday, Linda was sitting in our Six corner reading something. At first I thought it was an ordinary comic. Then I made a fantastic discovery.

'Brownies and Rainbows have their own special magazine. It's called *BROWNIE*, and it comes out once a month.'

'The first month Linda lent me her copy, but now I've ordered one for myself. I like the stories best (especially when they're about animals). Sue always starts with the puzzles, and Karen loves to try out the ideas for making things.'

What's that? Can I have a look?

'I wonder what you'll like best in *BROWNIE*? Why not borrow a copy from your Guider and find out?'

The Pow-wow Ring

Let's hold a Pow-wow.

A Pow-wow? What's that?

It's where we make plans.

Thinking caps on, Brownies. We need ideas for our next venture.

'A Venture is a sort of Brownie adventure.'

'We all thought hard and then Sue put three fingers into the circle – our Pack's secret sign showing she wanted to speak.'

◀ 'Soon everyone was making suggestions (one at a time, of course), and with some help from our Guiders, we planned something very exciting.'

Later, Emily will tell you more about that special Venture. Right now, you have something exciting to do. It's time to make your Brownie Guide Promise.

The Brownie Guide Promise

A Brownie gets ready to make her Promise in three ways.

She must hear or read the Brownie Story (so that she knows where the name Brownies came from).

She chooses the Brownie clothes she wants to wear.

She must understand the Promise and Law (because keeping the Promise and Law is what being a Brownie is all about).

The next part of your Handbook will help you get ready for your Promise. Start by looking through the Brownie Story, which starts over the page. If you can't read very well, don't worry. Just ask someone to read it to you, and you can follow the pictures.

let's get ready.

The Brownie Story

1 The cottage on the edge of the wood was in an awful mess. There were dishes to be washed, clothes to be ironed and toys scattered all over the floor.

2 Tommy and Betty didn't care. They hated boring old housework.

'What am I to do?' their mother sighed. 'I can't keep the cottage tidy. If only we had a Brownie!'

'What's a Brownie?' asked Tommy.

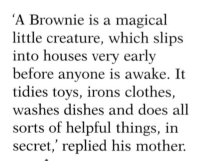

3 'A Brownie is a magical little creature, which slips into houses very early before anyone is awake. It tidies toys, irons clothes, washes dishes and does all sorts of helpful things, in secret,' replied his mother.

4 That's great! How can we get one?' Betty wondered.

5 'The Wise Owl in the wood would know, I suppose,' her mother said.

6 Late that night, Tommy and Betty crept out of the cottage into the wood. It was cold and dark and full of shadows. Or were they ghosts?

'We can't go back. We've got to find the Wise Owl,' said Betty firmly.

7 'Twitt twoo. How do you do?' a voice hooted at them from a nearby tree.

8 'The Wise Owl!' Tommy hugged Betty in relief. And soon the children were seated on a branch, snuggling close to the big bird's feathers.

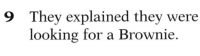

9 They explained they were looking for a Brownie.

'Do you know where we could find one?' asked Betty.

'Indeed I do,' hooted the Owl, and, placing her beak close to Betty's ear, she explained.

10 'Tommy, imagine!' exclaimed Betty. 'There's a Brownie in that pool over there. I've got to go to the pool, turn round three times and say:

"Twist me and turn me and show me the elf, I looked in the water and there saw . . .".'

11 'Who? Who? Who?' hooted the Owl. 'Look into the water and you'll find your Brownie looking back at you. Her name will finish the rhyme.'

12 The children raced over to the pool. Betty did exactly as the Owl had said:

'Twist me and turn me and show me the elf, I looked in the water and there saw . . .' She looked into the pool.

13 'Well, can you see it? Can you see a Brownie?' yelled Tommy, hopping from foot to foot in excitement.

'No,' said Betty. 'All I can see is my own reflection.'

17 Tommy and Betty returned thoughtfully to the cottage. If you had passed that way very early next morning, you would have seen a lamp burning in the kitchen window and two figures busily scurrying about inside.

Early next morning

14 Tommy and Betty were so tired and so disappointed that by the time they reached the tree again, they were in tears.

'Boo, hoo hoo. What's the matter with you two?' hooted the Owl, offering them a hanky.

15 'We didn't find a Brownie,' sniffed Betty. 'I saw no one in the water but myself.'

'Well, well,' said the Owl. 'Let's see if *that* fits the rhyme.'

'Twist me and turn me and show me the elf, I looked in the water and there saw . . .'

16 'Myself!' finished Betty. 'But I'm not a Brownie!'

'Too true, too true,' hooted the Owl. 'But you could act like one for a change and so could Tommy. It would be fun.'

18 And when the children's mother came down for breakfast, she couldn't believe her eyes. There wasn't a toy in sight. Everything was clean and tidy.

'Why, a Brownie has been here. How wonderful!' she gasped.

Later

19 From that day to this, the cottage has been like a different place. And Tommy and Betty have been like different children. They never get bored now; they are so busy planning their secret Good Turns.

20 Of course, their mother has discovered the truth. She thinks she is very lucky to have such helpful children. And Tommy and Betty have discovered how right the Wise Owl was: being human Brownies is FUN!

The End

Being a Brownie is fun!

Now that you have read the Brownie Story you will understand:

where the name 'Brownie' came from

why some Brownie Packs place a pool at the centre of their Ring

why some Brownie Guiders are called Brown Owl

You may also be interested to know:

● make-believe Brownies were supposed to dance around toadstools, which is why some Packs have a toadstool at the centre of the Ring.

What I Wear for Brownies

Here is Linda in her Brownie clothes.

The clothes are mix-and-match, so you can choose what you want to wear.

I chose a polo shirt and sweat pants.

Brownies don't have to wear a hat, but Linda thinks her baseball cap is fun. Her Pack decided that they would wear neckerchiefs, so most weeks she puts on her yellow neckerchief too.

Instead of a polo shirt you might choose a T-shirt, a yellow sweatshirt or a dark brown Brownie sweater. You can wear a pair of Brownie culottes with a belt instead of sweat pants.

Brownies aim to look smart and feel comfortable in what they wear.

Sometimes Linda wears her Brownie sash. The tape with the name of her Pack is sewn lengthwise on the shoulder, and underneath is her Pixie emblem. She has sewn on the rest of her badges where she wants.

As soon as you make your Promise you get your Promise Badge. This can be worn on your sash or on some other part of your top. In fact you can pin your Promise Badge to whatever clothes you are wearing.

Don't forget to mark your name on what you choose. You don't want to end up in someone else's sweater!

Brownie clothes make you feel you belong. But the way you really become a Brownie is by making your Promise.

The Brownie Guide Promise

What does a Promise mean? Here's an example.

Emily wanted one of her Six to wait for her after Brownies.

Helen said, 'I might wait.'

I might wait.

And Karen said, 'I'll probably wait.'

I'll probably wait.

But it wasn't until Sue said, 'I promise I'll wait,' that Emily was content. Why? Because Sue had used those two important words, 'I promise'; so Emily knew she would be there.

I promise I'll wait.

When we promise something we are telling people that we really mean to do what we say.

Once you understand how important a promise is, you are ready to look at the special Promise made by Brownie Guides. Brownies all over the world make a Promise like this.

I'll help you learn the words.

The Brownie Guide Promise

I promise that I will do my best:
To love my God,
To serve the Queen and my country,
To help other people
and
To keep the Brownie Guide Law.

Do you remember why Brownies make the Brownie Guide sign with three fingers? It's because the Promise has three parts.

A Brownie needs to know not only the words of her Promise, but also what each part means. She does not want to be like the girl who was asked to bring her brother's favourite comic back from town.

'I promise I will,' she said.

But when she reached the shop and saw all the different comics, she felt silly. She'd forgotten to find out the name of his favourite, so she didn't know which one to buy.

Promising something, without thinking about it first, can lead to problems.

That's why every sensible Brownie spends some time thinking about each part of her Promise before she makes it.

Let's think about the first part now:

I promise that I will do my best:

To love my God

Friendship

Sharing

Lending a Hand

Hunger

Loneliness

Greed

When a Brownie promises to love her God, she is saying she will try to live like the people in the top picture, and try to stop the things in the bottom picture.

How else can Brownies love their God?

Here are some Brownies keeping the first part of their Promise.

'I give thanks for everything I have been given – my home, my food, my family and my friends.'

'I talk or pray to God about the things which happen to me each day.'

'I say sorry to God when I've done something wrong.'

'I try to learn more about God week by week.'

Your Promise goes on to underline something God asks every Brownie to do, which is...

To serve the Queen and my country

'I can't serve the Queen. I don't live anywhere near Buckingham Palace,' a new Brownie was once heard to wail. She was happy to find that serving the Queen didn't mean washing Palace windows or vacuuming Palace carpets.

She could keep the second part of her Promise without leaving her home town.

Can you think how?

The answer is quite simple really. Our Queen works hard to make our country and all the countries of which she is Queen or Head happy places for people to live. Serving the Queen means helping her with this work. It means looking round your area to see what needs to be done. Is there litter in the park? Are there old people who feel lonely?

If you were to ask these Brownies what they were doing, they might say, 'We're visiting our friends in Riverside House,' and that answer would be right. But they could also say, 'We're serving the Queen,' and that answer would be right too.

When Brownies help other people they serve the Queen and their country at the same time. So this joins up with the third part of the Promise, which is . . .

To help other people and to keep the Brownie Guide Law.

The third part of your Promise can begin in your own home. There are lots of ways to help there.

The Brownie Guide Law is all about helping people.

The Brownie Guide Law

A Brownie Guide thinks of others before herself and does a Good Turn every day.

Sometimes keeping the Law is easy.

But keep trying to spot new ways to Lend a Hand. Helping people without being asked is what makes Brownie Good Turns special.

Sometimes it is very difficult.

We're always ready to help!

The Brownie Guide Promise Ceremony

Emily has been coming to Brownies for four weeks now. She knows the words of the Promise and the Law, and understands them. She knows what making her Brownie Promise will mean.

This is what happens at Emily's Promise ceremony.

The Pack makes a circle round the Brownie toadstool. Linda, Emily's Sixer, takes her by the hand. Together they skip into the centre where Mrs James is waiting.

Emily stands facing her Guider.

'Yes,' replies Emily.

'Emily, this is an important day,' says Mrs James. 'You are ready to make your Promise.

'Do you know that if you make the Promise, you must always do your best to keep it everywhere, every day, and especially at home?'

'Now make your Promise as a Brownie Guide.'

◀ Emily says her Promise. She makes the Brownie Guide sign as she speaks. So do the rest of the Pack.

'I promise that I will do my best: to love my God, to serve the Queen and my country, to help other people and to keep the Brownie Guide Law,' says Emily.

'What is the Brownie Guide Law?' asks Mrs James.

'A Brownie Guide thinks of others before herself and does a Good Turn every day.'

'Emily, I trust you to keep your Promise,' replies Mrs James. 'Welcome to the Pack!' she says with a big smile.

Then the whole Pack gives Emily a Pack Salute, and Emily feels very hot, relieved and very pleased with herself all at once.

I'm a real Brownie now!

Are you ready to make your Promise, too? Your Pack is looking forward to welcoming you.

The way they do it may be slightly different to the way Emily's Pack welcomed her, but the Promise ceremony will be exactly the same.

Don't forget.

Do you remember seeing Freda? You've already seen her three times. Freda the elephant never forgets. She's there to remind you about your Promise.

The Brownie Guide Promise Badge

Here is a close-up view of the Promise Badge you will receive. ▶

Wearing the Badge shows that you have made your Promise.

The Badge is very like the ones worn by all the members of the Guide family in the United Kingdom. The colour shows that you are a Brownie Guide.

The three leaves of the trefoil stand for the three parts of the Promise. The star stands for the Law.

I made my Promise on

....

The World Badge

Did you know that in almost every country in the world you have Brownie sisters? (Millions of them!) Guides and Brownies everywhere wear a World Badge, which looks like this:

A Brownie Prayer

Because your Promise is so important it is a good idea to ask your God to help you to keep it.

Brownies in some Packs use the words of this prayer, starting and finishing in the way they find most comfortable.

Dear Father in Heaven,
We know we are your children.
We want to serve you faithfully;
We want to keep our Brownie Guide Promise.
Help us to listen to your voice;
Help us to be willing
And quick to do your work;
Help us to be friendly and loving;
And help us to thank you every day
For all your gifts to us.
Amen.

Any Questions ?

On the following pages are answers to questions new Brownies often ask:

Question
'How did Brownies begin?'

Answer

In 1908, a man called Lord Baden-Powell ('B-P') had the wonderful idea which started Scouts and Guides. Many of the girls coming to Guides had small sisters. These younger girls saw all the interesting and exciting things Guides did. They wanted to join in. So B-P decided to start a group for them called the Rosebuds.

The Rosebuds loved their meetings, but soon it was clear that they didn't like their name. Lord Baden-Powell remembered a story he had heard about certain helpful, mischievous creatures . . . and as you've probably guessed, the Rosebuds have been Brownies ever since.

To begin with, the Rosebuds wore blue uniforms like the Guides, but later the colour of their uniform changed to match their name.

Question
'Our Guider said February 22nd was a sort of Guiding birthday. What did she mean?'

Answer

February 22nd was the birthday of both Lord Baden-Powell, the Founder of our Movement, and Olave, Lady Baden-Powell, his wife, who was the World Chief Guide. On this date every year, members of the Guide Movement all over the world have a day of celebration called Thinking Day.

On Thinking Day, everyone thinks about the World Guide Family. Often there are services and special Thinking Day meetings. Brownies pray for their sisters around the world. They also give money to help them, through the Thinking Day Fund.

They have a lot of fun too. Here are members of Emily's Pack wearing Brownie clothes from other countries for a Thinking Day party. Can you find out which countries they are from?

Answer

Every Brownie Pack has expenses. Money is needed to buy badges, books and equipment. It is also needed for Good Turns and Ventures – to hire a bus, for example, or to buy biscuits for a Parents' Evening. The Brownie hall can cost money, too; many Packs pay some money for heat and light.

Every Pack also sends money each year to Commonwealth Headquarters in London to help keep the whole Guide Association running smoothly.

So you can see how important it is to remember your subscription. With all these expenses, every penny counts.

42

Brownie Activities

Now that you're a real Brownie, I'm going to tell you about the special things Brownies do.

Interest Badges

BROWNIE GUIDES

Brownie Journeys and Challenges

BROWNIE FOOTPATH

LONDON 50 MILES

Pack Ventures

'As you can see from these pictures, Brownies sometimes work on their own, but very often the whole Pack will plan an activity and carry it out together. We call that a Pack Venture.'

Some Pack Ventures are big...

Some are indoors . . .

Some are small . . .

Hooray!

Welcome Princess Margaret

Some are special . . .

Some are simply fun!

BROWNIE FLOAT

Some are outdoors . . .

SPONSORED WEED

Some are hard work . . .

But whatever the Venture, we must remember that each of us, from the smallest to the tallest, is needed.

'There'll be a special part for YOU in your Pack Ventures. Can you think of something that you are good at? Something that you enjoy doing?

'In my Six . . .

'Linda always has lots of ideas.

'Karen can sew and knit and write very neatly.

'Jill is good at drawing and painting.

'Helen runs like the wind and knows how to ride.

'Sue is always smiling and friendly. She's really good at tidying up.

'EVERYONE is good at something.

'So when we go on Ventures we work together with all the other Brownies in our Pack to make the Venture a success.'

The Story of our Latest Venture

'Look back to page 18. Our Venture began in the Pow-wow Ring. Sue told us about an Indian village she had seen on TV. "The women who live there have to walk miles each day to fetch water," she said. "They really need their own well. Could we lend a hand to make one?"

'"We could send money," suggested Kate. "But how can we get it?"

'There were lots of ideas, then Linda asked, "What about a pet show? We could enter our pets and invite Brownies from the other side of town!"'

'This is the invitation we sent. Jill designed it.'

2nd Hammington
Brownie Pack
Invites you
to a
PET SHOW
for India
Saturday 2nd April
3.30 pm
Hammington School
Playground
Admission 50p

The following week

'The next week, we made lots of rosettes as prizes out of red, blue and yellow tissue paper.'

'I'll be delighted to be the judge.'

'We asked Mr Barnes, the vet, to act as judge.'

'A few weeks later we got a letter from the Fund organiser. "Drilling has begun and soon the village will have its new well," said Mrs James.

'We all cheered. What a great Venture!'

'Hooray!!'

The next Saturday

'On the day, the school playground was full of animals – dogs, cats, rabbits, goldfish … Kate even brought her pony and gave rides.

'Any Brownies without pets had the job of announcing the classes. By five o'clock the judging was over and the Sixers were able to count the money. "We've almost fifty pounds to send to the Fund," Linda shrieked.'

'Remembering special Ventures is fun. Actually, some of the Ventures I showed you on page 44 happened before I joined our Pack. I heard about them from Linda. Why not ask your Guider or one of the older Brownies to tell you what your Pack has done?'

The Venture Badge

'Have you seen anyone with a badge like this on her sash? It's called a Venture Badge and shows that the wearer has done her best in a Pack Venture.

'After our pet show every Brownie in the Pack was wearing one. We hadn't all done the same things. It was Linda who had the idea, and Jill who designed the invitation, but we all helped make rosettes. Even more important, we all turned up on the day. And afterwards, when the visitors had left, we all stayed behind to tidy up.'

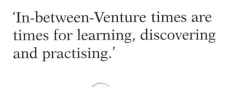
'In-between-Venture times are times for learning, discovering and practising.'

'Our Pack isn't working on a Venture right now, but that doesn't mean I've got nothing to do.

'I want to become a really experienced Brownie, carrying out my Promise in bigger, more adventurous ways.

'I want to be a really good Brownie, trying new things and practising them.'

'This is where Brownie Journeys and Interest Badges come in.'

Interest Badges

'Here is a Brownie Interest Badge.'

'Can you guess what it is given for? Yes, for good drawings and paintings. It's the Artist Badge.

'There are over fifty of these badges altogether, each awarded for a different interest and with a different picture in the centre. The *Brownie Guide Badge Book* explains all about them.'

'When you have made your Promise you can work for any Interest Badge you want.'

50

'After Jill designed the invitations for our pet show, she thought she would like to work for her Artist Badge. She asked Mrs James about it (you should always ask your Guider before beginning a badge), and together they looked it up in the *Brownie Guide Badge Book* to see what she had to do.'

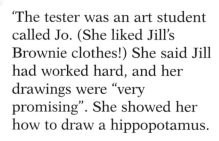

'For the next few weeks, Jill was very busy drawing and colouring in her spare time. Then, when the work was finished, Mrs James arranged for her test.'

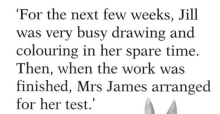

'The tester was an art student called Jo. (She liked Jill's Brownie clothes!) She said Jill had worked hard, and her drawings were "very promising". She showed her how to draw a hippopotamus.

'Jill passed her test, and was given an Artist Badge to sew onto her badge sash.'

'Linda's first Interest Badge was the Swimmer Badge. She did it as one of the Journey Challenges. I'll be telling you about those in a moment.'

'Now she has MILLIONS of badges!'

Well over ten, anyway!

'Next, with lots of other Brownies, she worked for her Walking Badge, as part of a Pack Venture.'

'But Mrs James says, "The best Brownie is the Brownie who tries hardest to keep her Promise, not the one with the most badges. The best reason for doing an Interest Badge is to learn a new way of helping others."'

Brownie Journeys and Challenges

Now that Emily has made her Promise, Mrs James says that she is ready to start her Footpath Journey.

'A journey! Will I be back by bedtime?' Emily asks Mrs James.

'It's an imaginary journey, not a real one,' smiles her Guider. 'There are three Brownie Journeys. Because you're seven, you'll start with the Footpath. Later you'll do your Road and then your Highway Journey. On each Journey there will be eight Challenges to try. You'll have to try harder the further you go.'

'What is a Challenge?' Emily wonders.

'If you can do something without any effort . . . then it ISN'T a real Challenge.' ▶

'A real Challenge isn't easy.' ▼

'It means practising and doing your very best. That's the way to improve.'

The Brownie Footpath

Here are Brownies journeying along the Brownie Footpath, working on eight different Challenges.

Brownies are wide awake

Brownies keep healthy

Brownies are friendly

Brownies help at home

Brownies lend a hand

Brownies do their best

Brownies make things

Brownies have fun out-of-doors

It doesn't matter which Challenge they do first. A Brownie on a Brownie Journey decides on the order with her Guider.

Are YOU ready to travel with Emily along the Brownie Footpath?

I'll be with you on your journey.

The next part of our Handbook tells you about each of the eight Challenges you will meet. There are charts and spaces which you can use to record your progress. Once you and your Guider are satisfied that you have completed a Challenge, you may colour in a square on the Brownie Footpath on page 74.

Then, when all eight sections are coloured in, you will have reached the end of your Journey, and will receive your Brownie Footpath Badge.

You will find hints on how to go about some of the Challenges at the back of your Handbook.

Look out for Freda as you travel. She's still there to remind you of your Promise.

Always remember to think of other people first and try to turn Challenges into Good Turns.

Brownies are Wide Awake

It's good to be Wide Awake! When you walk around in a day-dream you can miss all kinds of interesting and important things.

Choose at least one of the five Wide Awake Challenges on these pages and carry it out; or, if you prefer, you can think up a new Wide Awake Challenge of your own.

A Colour in a balloon each time you remember to bring your Handbook to Brownies and take it home again. Sometimes you will be asked to bring something special to a meeting. If you remember, draw in another balloon.

B Find out the name of each of these badges. Draw a badge you would like to try.

....

....

....
....
....

C Your eyes, ears, hands, nose and tongue can tell you a lot. Join the dots to create this picture which shows your senses (touching, listening, tasting, looking and smelling). What do you like to see, hear, touch, smell and taste? Write about it here:

I like to see..

I like to touch ....

I like to hear...

I like to smell..

I like to taste...

D Know your correct address, including the post code. Write it out on this envelope.

(Emily has written out her address on page 132 to help you.)

Are you on the telephone?
Do you know your number?
Write it here:

....

E Draw a ring around the dangers in this picture. Name five
ways in which you can stop accidents at home.

....

....

....

....

....

...OR

complete your Wide Awake Challenge in some other way.

Every Sunday, Emily travels by bus to visit her gran. She has found a way of keeping Wide Awake on the journey. She counts animals. The first time she did this she saw three hens, six dogs, two cats, eleven fields full of cows, four fields full of sheep and a rabbit. Afterwards she drew pictures of them, and Mrs James agreed that she had completed her Wide Awake Challenge.

When you have completed your Wide Awake Challenge, write about it or draw a picture of it in this box.▼

My Wide Awake Challenge

Brownies Keep Healthy

Your body is like a machine. Keep it working well, inside and out.
Choose and do one Challenge from EACH section. One section is about your body, the other is about exercise.

Body

A Match the parts of the body with the jobs they do.

You can find out more about how your body works by looking at page 139.

B Eat some fresh fruit or vegetables each day for a week to keep your body fit and healthy. Draw what you liked best.▼

Brain

Digesting and absorbing food

Filtering blood and producing urine

Breathing

Heart

Lungs

Thinking

Stomach and intestine

Pumping blood

Kidneys

C Make a special effort to look after your nails, teeth or hair for one week (see page 140 for advice). Write down or draw how you did this.

Keep it up!

Emily likes apples, but for her Keep Healthy Challenge she decided to try some different fruits. Here she is eating one of them. Do you know what it is? Have you ever eaten one?

···OR

keep your body healthy in some other way.

Exercise

A Play a skipping game with your Six using a long rope.

B Play a game like sevens, hopscotch or jump the blob. (The rules are on page 141.)

C Learn to hit a small ball up in the air with a racquet or bat for ten hits. Try to do it without missing.

D Make a target. How far away from the target can you sit or stand and still hit it with a ball or bean bag?

E Holding a ball or a float in your arms, use your legs to swim a width of the pool. Can you hold the ball or the float between your legs and use your arms to swim the same distance?

···OR

challenge yourself with any other way of keeping fit.

When you have completed your Keep Healthy Challenge, write about it or draw a picture of it in this box. ▼

My Keep Healthy Challenge

Brownies Do Their Best

As a Brownie, you will always be trying to do your best, but these Challenges will help you to learn more about your Promise.

Choose and do one of these Challenges.

A Collect pictures of things for which you would like to thank God. Use them to decorate a prayer card or a thank-you card.

B Copy the Brownie Law and decorate it for your Six corner, box or table, or for your bedroom or noticeboard at home.

C Make a collage about smiling and remember to use your Brownie smile.

D Tidy your toys, books and games so that you can always find what you are looking for.

E Take part in a Good Turn Venture with your Pack.

…OR

do your best in some other way to help someone.

When you have done your best, write about it or draw a picture of it in this box. ▼

I did my best by…

DO Your Best!

Brownies Make Things

Brownies can make toys and decorations with their hands, and they can make stories and poems in their heads. They can make a story come to life by acting it, miming it or even singing it.

Choose and do one of these Challenges.

A Make a greetings card or decoration at or for a Brownie event or to celebrate a festival. (You can find one idea on page 156.)

B Using natural materials make a present. (There are some ideas on page 157.) Who will you give it to?

C Make a model of Freda the elephant. You can use any materials – marzipan, clay, junk, felt or pompoms, for example.

D Make a toy or game for someone who is younger than you or ill at home. (You will find one idea on page 158.)

E With your Brownie friends, tell a story and use sound effects – you could use your voice, musical instruments or other objects.

...OR

make anything else you choose.

For my Making Things Challenge I made

. . . .

. . . .

Draw a picture of it here. ▼

Put a tick in this box if you tidied up afterwards. ☐

Brownies are Friendly

Brownies start by being friendly with the members of their own Six and go on to discover Brownie friends all over the world.

Choose and do one of these Challenges.

Being friendly is fun!

A Choose a different partner for each game you play or activity you do at Brownies over a two-week period.

B Play a game or sing a song from another country. Find out three facts about that country.

C Tell, read or hear a story from a country where there are Brownies. When you know the story, act it out with a group of Brownie friends.

D Find out why 22nd February is special in Guiding (see page 41). Take part in a Thinking Day activity.

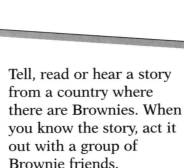

···OR

work out another Being Friendly Challenge with your Guider.

When you have completed your Being Friendly Challenge, write about it or draw a picture of it in the box above.

Brownies Lend a Hand

The more you know, the better you will be able to Lend a Hand.

Make Freda a happy elephant. Here's how:

Remember to do a different Good Turn every day for one week and draw or write about it in the Elephant House. ▶

Also, choose and do one Challenge.

A Know what to do if you have a simple burn and what to do if someone's clothes are on fire. (You can find out about this on page 173.) Show your Guider what you would do.

B Know how to use, carry and pass scissors and knives (see page 177). Show your Guider how you would do one of these things. How do you open tins at home? Can you do this safely, too?

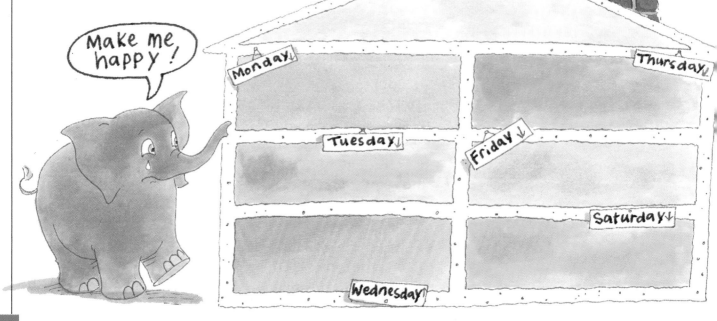

Make me happy!

Sunday

Monday

Thursday

Tuesday

Friday

Saturday

Wednesday

C Take on a special job at your meeting place for at least three weeks.

Emily's job was sorting out the Pack equipment box. Mrs James showed her how to tie the skipping ropes to stop them getting tangled.

D Show a younger child how to tie shoe laces, do up a coat, fasten a watch strap, plait hair or do something similar.

···OR

make up your own Lend a Hand Challenge.

When you have completed your Lend a Hand Challenge, write about it or draw a picture of it in this box.▼

My Lend a Hand Challenge

Brownies Help at Home

There are lots of different ways to help at home. **Choose and do one of the Challenges suggested below.**

A Empty, clean and re-line a kitchen waste bin.

B Show that you can hang out and take in washing and fold it ready for ironing. (You can find out how to do this on page 180.)

C Learn how to fold clothes and pack them in a travel bag or suitcase. (Page 181 tells you how to do this.)

D Prepare two different sorts of fresh vegetables for cooking.

E Lay a place setting for a meal in your home. (Look at page 182 to find out how to do this.) Clear away afterwards and stack the dishes ready for washing.

F Clean boots or shoes that need polishing. (One way to do this is described on page 182.)

My Help at Home Challenge

G Clean a shower, bath or sink (see page 183).

···OR

do some other helpful job.

When you have completed your Help at Home Challenge, write about it or draw a picture of it in this box.

keep busy!

Brownies Have Fun Out-of-doors

There are wonderful things to discover and enjoy in nature. **Choose and do one of these outdoor Challenges.**

A Choose a small area outside and put out scraps of food. Sit quietly for a time and watch what comes to visit it.

B Clean the mud off dirty wellingtons and boots. Put what you have collected in a pot, water it and see what grows!

C Name and draw three birds, flowers, trees, fish, insects or butterflies, or three different sorts of buildings which you have seen, and find out something about them.

D Find a spider's web and study it carefully. Draw the pattern you see and find out something about spiders and their webs. (There are some facts about spiders on page 192.)

E Follow a trail which has been laid in wool, string or some other material.

···OR

enjoy yourself out-of-doors in some other way.

When you have completed your Out-of-doors Challenge, write about it or draw a picture of it in this box. ▶

This is what Karen wrote about her Out-of-doors Challenge:

> I found a spider's web in the garden shed. It was in the window frame. The spider had caught some insects in its silky web.

My Out-of-doors Challenge

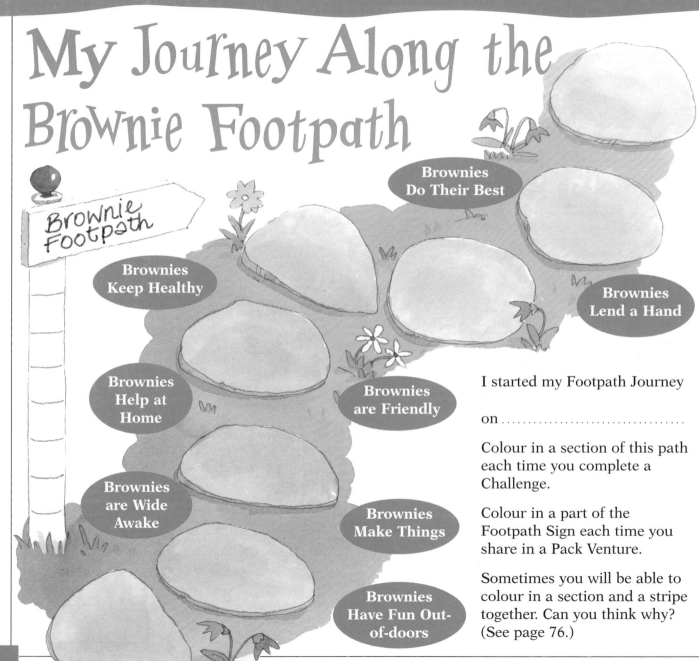

My Journey Along the Brownie Footpath

Brownie Footpath

Brownies Do Their Best

Brownies Keep Healthy

Brownies Lend a Hand

Brownies Help at Home

Brownies are Friendly

Brownies are Wide Awake

Brownies Make Things

Brownies Have Fun Out-of-doors

I started my Footpath Journey

on ....

Colour in a section of this path each time you complete a Challenge.

Colour in a part of the Footpath Sign each time you share in a Pack Venture.

Sometimes you will be able to colour in a section and a stripe together. Can you think why? (See page 76.)

Now you have reached the end of the Brownie Footpath.

And look who's here!

Hi there!

How I kept my Promise by Emily

This Journey helped me to keep my Promise better. I try to remember my Brownie smile – even when Mum tells me it's bedtime. This is doing my best. I also remember to say thank you to God.

On this Journey I cleaned the bath and tidied the Brownie equipment box and did not fight with Sophie in the bus because I was wideAwake counting animals. This is helping other people, especially my Mum.

Well done!

Freda is always very keen to meet Brownies at the end of a Journey.

She likes them to look back over what they have learned and to think how they have kept their Promise.

Emily did this, and then she wrote her answer down.

You may not feel able to put your answer on paper, but Freda will be quite happy if you chat it over with your Guider.

Once you have done this, you will receive your Brownie Footpath Badge.

The Challenge that Grew

For her Making Things Challenge Karen made a Christmas decoration. It was so pretty that the other Brownies wanted to make one too.

How did you do it?

I'd like to try that.

It's lovely!

'Could we have a Christmas decoration-making Venture?' Emily asked.

'That's a good idea!' Mrs James agreed.

'We could take some decorations round to the old people's flats where my Nan and Grandpa live,' said Linda.

'And sing carols for them,' added Sue.

Challenges grow into Ventures as easily as that.

And during a Venture Brownies often find themselves completing a Challenge.

The Brownie Birthday Badge

For every year you spend as a Brownie, like Emily, you will receive a Birthday Badge. The first Birthday Badge is yellow, the second is green and the third is red.

It's exactly one year since Emily made her Brownie Promise. Today, at the meeting, she is celebrating her Brownie Birthday. Of course, she isn't getting presents like she did for her ordinary birthday last month, but it is still a special occasion. Mrs James has presented her with her first Brownie Birthday Badge. Linda has given her a card from her Six. (It has a copy of the Promise inside.) And the whole Pack gives her a Pack Salute.

It's like having my Promise ceremony all over again.

A Brownie wears her Birthday Badge on her badge sash, and each year she replaces the old badge with the new one.

Position of Badges

On her sash Emily now has her Footpath Badge and her Brownie Birthday Badge. She has also been working for her Animal Lover Badge. Have you started working for your first Interest Badge yet?

Here is a close-up view of a Brownie wearing her badge sash, showing where she has sewn her different badges.

Footpath Badge
Road Badge
Highway Badge

Sixer/Second stripe

Promise Badge

Brownie Birthday Badge

Venture Badge

Interest Badges

Sash clip

Pack name tape

Rainbow Badge

Six Emblem

County or Country Badge

World Badge

Brownie Revels

Emily has just been to her first Brownie Revels and can't wait to tell you all about it.

'This is the invitation our Guider read out in our last Pow-wow. I couldn't believe it. Robin Hood inviting me to a party!

'Then Mrs James explained that our Pack had been invited to Brownie Revels. Lots of other Packs had been invited, too, because that's what Revels are all about. They give Brownies from different Packs a chance to do something together. You never quite know what that something will be.

'On the Saturday of our Revels, Hammington Forest became Sherwood Forest for three hours. The Guiders dressed up. (Can you spot Mrs James?) We had an opening ceremony, played lots of games and finished off with a banquet of crisps and orange juice in the Sheriff of Nottingham's Castle.'

Robin Hood invites all the Brownies of the District to a party with Maid Marian and the Merry Men at Hammington Forest Park on Saturday 28th May at 3pm.

Ideas for Ventures

'I wonder what your first Brownie Revels will be like? One thing is for sure – you will be having fun with Brownies you have never met before. So don't just talk to members of your own Pack. Brownie Revels are a great way of making friends!

'I asked three Brownies I met at our Brownie Revels to tell me their latest Ventures. This is what they said.'

'My Pack held Spring Sports. We moved round different activities in our Sixes. We found out who was the champion in each activity and we all got points for doing our best.'

'My Pack had a Friendship Venture. We filled a scrapbook with information about ourselves. We sent it to a Brownie Pack in Canada. Now we're looking forward to getting a scrapbook back from them.'

'Our last Venture was a visit to the fire station. We saw inside a fire engine. A fireman talked to us about safety in the home and taught us how to make an emergency 'phone call.'

...Pack Holiday

'Perhaps you're wondering why we have so much luggage with us. It's because we're about to set off on the most exciting Brownie Venture of all . . .'

'A Pack Holiday is a holiday Brownies spend together with their Pack; sleeping together, eating together, working together and playing together.

'For our last Pack Holiday, we went to a big Brownie House near the sea. Every day different Sixes helped with the chores – cleaning, cooking and washing up – so we were able to practise lots of skills we'd learnt on our Journeys, and to try new Challenges as well.

'We played games, went on expeditions and did all sorts of other things. What I enjoyed most was the story last thing at night, and Jill loved the pyjama party!

'By the way, Brownies on Pack Holiday don't go around in their pyjamas all the time. We usually wear our Brownie clothes and take along some spare things in the same colours.'

Your Second Brownie Journey

On the opposite page you will find a map of your second Brownie Journey. It is along a road this time. As you travel you will meet another eight Challenges. Just as a road tends to be bigger than a footpath, so these Challenges will be bigger than the ones you completed last year.

Once you and your Guider agree that you have finished them all, you will receive your Brownie Road Badge.

Of course, you won't be making the Journey alone. Guiders are always there to give help and advice, and you will find hints on some Challenges at the back of this Handbook. You will probably be able to carry out some Challenges with other Brownies as part of a Pack Venture.

Don't forget about me!

You wouldn't, would you? As you make this Brownie Journey, you'll remember your Promise.

So, when you're ready, take a look at . . .

ROAD
3
BROWNIE GUIDES

...The Brownie Road

Things you do along the Brownie Road may make you want to work for an Interest Badge. Draw pictures of Interest Badges you'd like to try on your Journey.

You don't *have* to get six!!

You will find lots of ideas for Interest Badges, Journey Challenges and Ventures in your magazine – *BROWNIE.*

Brownies are Wide Awake

On the Brownie Footpath you learnt to notice what was going on around you. Now you can practise remembering things as well. Make sure that you put your noticing and remembering to good use! Choose and do one of these Challenges.

A Use a public telephone to telephone someone you know. You will need a card or some coins. Pass on a clear message. Describe to your Guider how to contact the emergency services. (For help, see pages 132-134.)

B Know the rules of the road when out walking. The Green Cross Code is on page 134. Explain to a Footpath Brownie how to cross the road safely.

C Sharpen your memory. First, remember a tune, song or poem and then hum, sing or say it to your Six. Also, invent a memory game and play it with your Six.

challenge yourself to notice and remember in some other way.

When you have completed your Wide Awake Challenge, write about it or draw a picture of it in this box.▼

My Wide Awake Challenge

D Know how to get help in an emergency at home (see page 134).

Emily keeps all sorts of useful 'phone numbers in her 'Emergency Telephone Numbers' book. So when the washing machine overflowed, she raced upstairs to get it. 'Lucky we don't need the doctor, the vet or the coastguard this time, Mum,' she said. 'Just ring Hammington 600 for a plumber.'

Brownies Keep Healthy

Looking after our bodies and taking exercise are two of the ways to keep healthy. Choose and do one Challenge from EACH section.

Body

A Find out which foods help to keep your body healthy. (There is some information on page 142.) Then plan a healthy meal you would enjoy eating.

B Discover why it is important to visit the dentist regularly. Make a poster to encourage people to do this.

C Make a chart showing what time you went to bed each night for a week and what time you got up. How do you feel when you don't get enough sleep?

Why are sleeping and relaxing important to health? Help your Guiders and the Pack to enjoy five minutes' relaxation.

D Look in a chemist's shop or collect advertisements to find the names or types of different soaps, shampoos or toothpastes. How are they different? Why is it important to rinse after using them? What do the Brownies in your Pack use?

... OR

challenge yourself to look after your body in another way.

Exercise

A Take part in a sport such as swimming, dancing, short tennis, gymnastics or football and show how you have improved over at least one month.

B Walk a little extra every day for one week. Perhaps you could walk a dog with an adult, or walk to school, or while you are at school walk around the playground during break times.

C Make up a game using a bat and ball and play it with your Six.

D Stand straight with your back against a wall. Hold out your arms in front of you and bend your knees. See if you can do this with a book on your head. Put the book on the floor and pick it up using the same movement. Learn the correct way to lift heavy objects and show the Pack (see page 143).

...OR

think up an Exercise Challenge to do yourself.

When you have completed your Keep Healthy Challenge, write about it or draw a picture of it in this box. ▶

As you know Helen is very athletic. After doing her Keep Healthy Exercise Challenge she decided to work for her Agility Badge. She looked at the *Brownie Guide Badge Book* with Mrs James, practised hard and passed her test with flying colours.

My Keep Healthy Challenge

Brownies Do Their Best

 As a Brownie, you will always be trying to do your best, but these Challenges will help you to learn more about your Promise.

Choose and do one of the Challenges below.

A Write a list or draw pictures of the things that are important to you. Tell your Six why you have chosen those things.

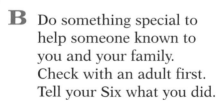

B Do something special to help someone known to you and your family. Check with an adult first. Tell your Six what you did.

C Be kind to someone whom you know but who is not your best friend. What does it really mean to be a friend to someone?

D Make a small part of this world more beautiful by planting a few seeds, collecting some litter or something similar.

E Find out why countries have national anthems, when they are used and how you should behave while they are being sung or played. Learn one verse of the national anthem of your country. (The words of the National Anthem of the United Kingdom are on page 150.)

···OR

do your best in some other way.

When you have done your best, write about it or draw a picture of it in this box. ▶

I did my best by···

Emily Does Her Best

When Emily was on the Brownie Footpath, she did her best by remembering her Brownie smile – even when her mum said it was bedtime.

On the Brownie Road she tried to do her best in a bigger way. There was a new girl in her class who seemed shy and lonely. Emily made a special effort to be friendly.

A few weeks later she told Mrs James what she had done.

'I picked Sunita as my partner for games, and every break-time we had a chat.'

'Good for you! That certainly shows you were keeping your Promise – helping someone to settle in,' the Guider approved.

'There's just one problem,' Emily frowned. 'I don't feel as if I'm doing my best any more. I mean, Sunita's a real friend now. She helps me every bit as much as I help her.'

'That's not a problem, Emily,'

Well done, Emily! The best way to make friends is to be one.

smiled Mrs James. 'Brownies who do their best make all sorts of important discoveries. You've just found out something about friendship.'

Brownies Make Things

Brownies on the Brownie Road try to make something they haven't already made on the Footpath.

Choose and do one of these Challenges.

A Make a decoration for a table. (For one idea look at page 162.)

B Write a letter to *BROWNIE* magazine. (You will need to ask your Guider how to send it.)

C Make and decorate something useful to use at Brownies or perhaps on Pack Holiday, for example a sitter, a table mat, a bean bag, a soft ball, a cover for your Handbook, a draught excluder, a memo pad, a pencil holder, a small brush. (See pages 159-161 for some ideas.)

D Make a glove puppet or a set of finger puppets and use them to act out a well-known story. (Some ideas on making puppets are on pages 162-164.)

···OR

make up something else of your own choice.

Write about what you have done in this scroll. ▼

E Listen to a piece of music and talk to your Guider about it.

Brownies are Friendly

Being friendly means being interested in other people – meeting them and finding out about them.

Choose and do one of these Challenges.

A Start your own Six book or contribute to the Six book if your Six already has one. You could decorate the front of the book and ask each member of the Six to bring a photograph or draw a picture of herself. Write something interesting about each person or about an activity you have done as a Six.

B Join in an event with a group of Rainbows, Guides, Cub Scouts or Brownies from another Pack. (You will need to plan this with your Guider.)

C Make a friendship circle showing other members of the UK Guiding family (see page 170).

D Invite someone from another culture, or someone who has visited another country, to come to your Pack meeting to show everyone some food, a craft or a dance from that culture or country. (Notes on inviting and welcoming visitors are on page 171.)

E Find your own country on a world map. Copy its shape. Where in that country do you live? Mark the place on the map. Discover where three other members of your Pack have been and ask them to point out the places or countries on a map.

My Being Friendly Challenge

...OR

be friendly in some other way.

When you have completed your Being Friendly Challenge, write about it or draw a picture of it in the box above.

Sue went to the Brownie Revels in Hammington Forest Park. For her Brownie Road Challenge she wrote down some things she discovered about the Brownies she met.

My discoveries about others

I met a lot of Brownies from different packs. I met a Brownie called Sarah and a Brownie called Parveen. Their pack meets on a Thursday evening and Sarah is a Second. She has four Interest Badges. Parveen has a Friendship Badge. She said Brownies in Bangladesh are called Yellowbirds. Her family came from Bangladesh, but she was born in this country.

Brownies Lend a Hand

Now you are on the Brownie Road you are trusted to act sensibly. The more sensible (or responsible) you are, the better you will be able to Lend a Hand.

Remember to do a Good Turn every day and to do one of the following Challenges.

B Help in a garden for at least an hour in some of the following ways: weeding, planting, sweeping paths, raking leaves, tending a greenhouse, shovelling snow.

C Know how to tie a reef knot and know its uses. Learn one more knot and what it is used for. (Some knots are shown on page 179.)

D Learn how to take care of a bicycle (see page 178). Show an adult what you have done. Ask an adult to explain how the seat and handlebars are adjusted.

E Help prepare a room for a visitor.

This is the list Emily made when she was helping prepare a bedroom for her gran. ▼

A Tools need care and respect. Recognise two of the following tools and show that you can use them safely: hammer, screwdriver, pliers, saw, paintbrush, sandpaper. (There are some hints to help you on page 177.)

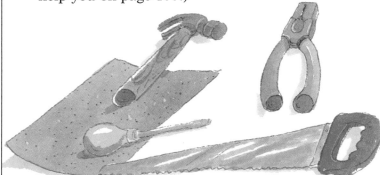

Put hangers in wardrobe.
Get clean towels from airing cupboard.
Clear out two drawers.
Polish mirror.
Put flowers in vase.

F Make a list of all the hazards around where you live or where your Brownie Pack meets.

···OR

Lend a Hand by helping in some other way.

When you have completed your Lend a Hand Challenge, write about it or draw a picture of it in this box. ▶

DO a Good Turn every day!

My Lend a Hand Challenge

Brownies Help at Home

In your home can you look after something or someone by yourself? On the Brownie Road you can learn some useful skills.

Choose and do one of these Challenges.

A Empty, clean and sort out a cupboard and return the contents neatly.

B Learn how to use a broom, a mop and bucket, a vacuum cleaner and a dustpan and brush.

C Do some simple sewing to include sewing on at least two of these items:

● a button
● a patch
● a name tape
● a Brownie badge.

(You will find some instructions on page 184.)

D Change the bedclothes on your bed (see page 185). Make your bed and keep your bedroom tidy for one week.

E Handwash socks, underwear or other small items of clothing (see page 180).

F Make a healthy snack and wash up afterwards.

G Make and serve tea or coffee for a visitor (see page 186). Wash up and tidy away afterwards.

···OR

help at home in some other way.

When you have completed your Help at Home Challenge, write about it or draw a picture of it in this box. ◀

Keep it up!

My Help at Home Challenge

Brownies Have Fun Out-of-doors

The more effort you put into a Challenge, the more you get out of it – particularly when you are out-of-doors!
Choose and do one of these Challenges.

A Look under a stone or log to see what life you can find there. Draw what you can see and try to identify it. (For some help, see page 191.)

B Go on a pond-dipping expedition or explore a rock pool with an adult you know. Find out how to keep safe beside water. Discover which creatures live on and under the water. (There is some information to help you on pages 192-194.)

C Set an adventure trail for your Guider and Pack. Make sure they have to use all their senses in order to follow the trail.

Emily's trail led down the main street, past some roadworks and an Indian restaurant, and on into the park. She gave Mrs James and some of the Brownies clues about what they'd see, hear, smell and touch to help them find their way.

D Invent an instrument to measure one aspect of the weather, such as the rain or wind. Use the instrument for one week and record your findings on a weather chart. (There are some ideas on pages 195-197.)

E Go on a short ramble with some Brownie friends. First check with your Guider and then ask an adult you know to go with you. Show that you know what to wear and what to pack in a daysac. (See pages 198-199 for hints on safe rambling.)

F Care for a pet for two weeks. (It need not be your own.) Keep a record of what you did for it.

···OR

think up an Out-of-doors Challenge of your own. (It may be linked to an Out-of-doors Venture.)

Answer these questions when you have completed your Challenge.

What did you do? ....

....

How long did it take? ....

What did you enjoy about it? ....

....

....

....

My Journey Along the Brownie Road

I started my Road Journey

on ....

Each time that you and your Guider agree that you have completed a Challenge, colour in a strip and write in the name of the Challenge on the Brownie Road.

Each time you share in a Pack Venture write what you did on a brick in the Venture Bridge.

Brownies Make Things

Brownies Keep Healthy

Brownies Help at Home

Brownies Do Their Best

Brownies are Wide Awake

Brownies are Friendly

Brownies Lend a Hand

Brownies Have Fun Out-of-doors

At the end of your second Brownie Journey, just as at the end of your first, it is a good idea to think about your Promise.

Serving the Queen and your country?

Helping other people?

Loving your God?

Have you discovered any new ways of keeping your Promise through the Challenges and Ventures you have done and the Interest Badges you have gained?

Try to spend a few moments chatting to your Guider about this. Perhaps she will be able to see your progress even more clearly than you can.

You are ready now to replace your Footpath Badge with the Brownie Road Badge.

Congratulations

Go! Challenges

This is the Go! Challenge Badge.

You can try Go! Challenges when you are nine.

You plan what you are going to do with your Guider, and then afterwards you'll talk about your adventures with the Pack.

Jill and Nicola have been working on Go! Challenges.

Nicola has designed a machine with moving parts. She's used card and rubber bands and bits of packaging. ▶

Jill has been finding out about how to care for her body. She's made some hand cream and learnt how to look after her nails.

Emily thinks they have both worked very hard, and everyone agrees they've done their best.

Pack Holiday Under Canvas

Emily is about to go on another Pack Holiday – this time under canvas. She has been finding out all about it from Linda, Karen and Helen who have now moved up to the Guides. Mrs James has asked Emily to become Sixer of the Gnomes, so we'll let Emily tell you what she has learnt.

'We're going to spend this year's holiday in tents on a camp site.

'We'll all help to put up the tents – one for each Six. Then we'll spend nearly a week in the open air. We'll help to cook meals and keep the camp site tidy and do lots more exciting things.

'What I'm looking forward to most is getting wood for the fire and telling stories in the tent at night.'

The Brownie Highway

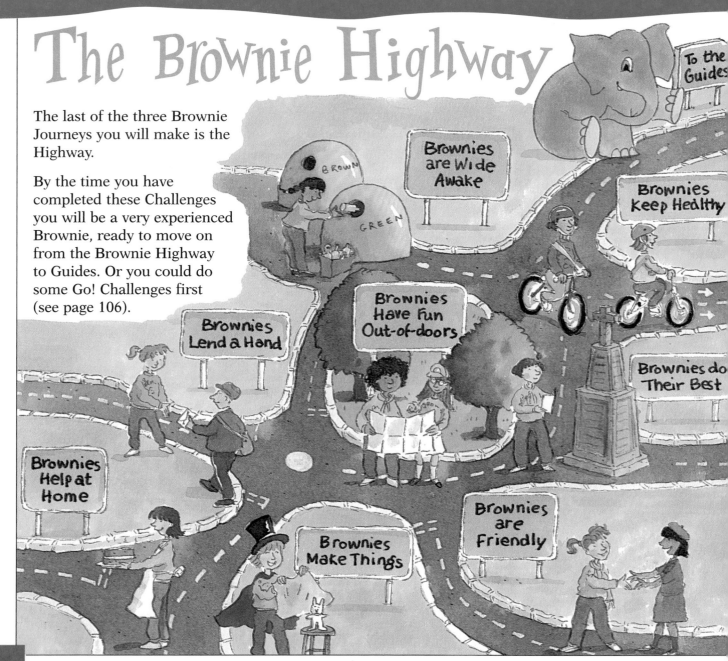

The last of the three Brownie Journeys you will make is the Highway.

By the time you have completed these Challenges you will be a very experienced Brownie, ready to move on from the Brownie Highway to Guides. Or you could do some Go! Challenges first (see page 106).

Brownies are Wide Awake

Brownies Keep Healthy

Brownies Lend a Hand

Brownies Have Fun Out-of-doors

Brownies do Their Best

Brownies Help at Home

Brownies Make Things

Brownies are Friendly

To the Guides

Brownies are Wide Awake

There are many interesting and important things which Brownies can learn about their surroundings.

Choose and do one of these Challenges.

A Find out what you can recycle in your area and where. Why is it important to recycle things? Encourage your Pack to collect something that can be recycled and take it to the local collection point. (See page 135 for some hints on recycling.)

B With your family, friends or school visit an interesting building or place near your home. Turn a plain white postcard into a picture postcard of the place you have visited with your own coloured drawing. Write a description on the back.

C Use a secret code to write a message to another Six. Give them the key to the code and see if they can decipher your message. There are some codes on pages 136-137, but you can make up your own, of course!

D Emily went shopping with Dad. When she got home she made a map of the supermarket. Make a map of your local shop or supermarket.

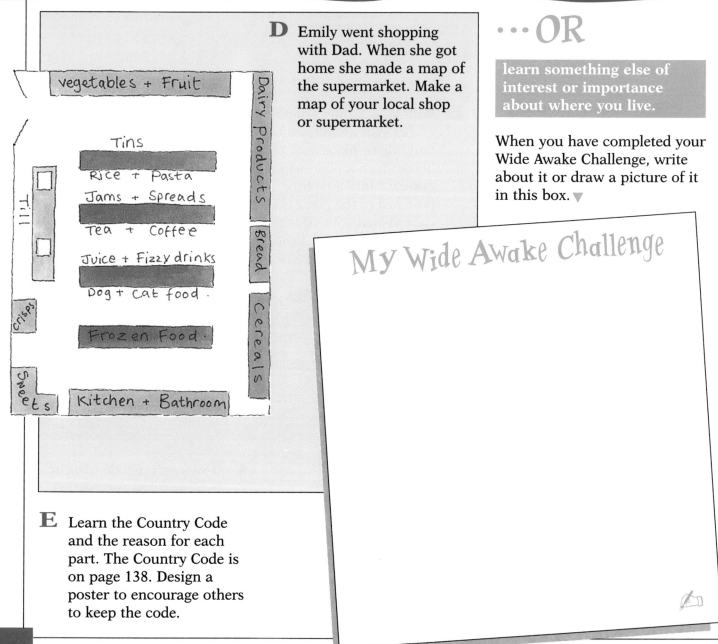

vegetables + Fruit

Dairy Products

Bread

Cereals

Tins

Rice + Pasta

Jams + Spreads

Tea + Coffee

Juice + Fizzy drinks

Dog + Cat food.

Frozen Food.

Till

Crisps

Sweets

Kitchen + Bathroom

E Learn the Country Code and the reason for each part. The Country Code is on page 138. Design a poster to encourage others to keep the code.

··· OR

learn something else of interest or importance about where you live.

When you have completed your Wide Awake Challenge, write about it or draw a picture of it in this box. ▼

My Wide Awake Challenge

Brownies Keep Healthy

 Your body keeps growing. You should learn what it needs to grow properly – and what can harm it.

Choose and do one Challenge from EACH section.

Body

A Some people need to use certain drugs every day to keep them well. Other people abuse their bodies by wrongly using solvents (such as glue), alcohol, cigarettes and harmful drugs. Find out how drugs, solvents, alcohol and tobacco can damage your body and make a poster warning people against the abuse of these things. (There is some information on page 144.)

B Make up a game to play with your Six or Pack which will help them learn about foods that are good and bad for healthy living. (There is some information about food on page 142.)

C Plan, make and eat a healthy packed lunch. Draw what you chose here. ▼

D Invite a mother to bring her baby to a Brownie meeting. Discover what things are good for the baby to keep it healthy. Find out how a mother can keep healthy while she is pregnant. (See page 145.)

···OR

show your Six another way
in which you have kept
your body healthy.

Exercise

A Go on a cycle ride with an adult you know. Remember to ask your mum or dad first. Don't forget to wear a helmet and a fluorescent safety strap, and always cycle safely. (There are some hints for doing this on page 149.) Tell your Six where you went. Why should your bicycle have your post code on it?

B Play rounders, French cricket (see page 145) or a similar team game. Find a playing position that you like, such as bowler, fielder, backstop or on a base. Practise to try to improve your game.

C Write your name with the hand you don't normally use. Then hold the pen between your toes and try to write your name again.

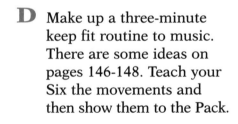

D Make up a three-minute keep fit routine to music. There are some ideas on pages 146-148. Teach your Six the movements and then show them to the Pack.

···OR

challenge yourself in some
other form of exercise.

When you have completed your Keep Healthy Challenge, write about it or draw a picture of it in the box above.

My Keep Healthy Challenge

Brownies Do Their Best

As a Brownie, you will always be trying to do your best, but these Challenges will help you to learn more about your Promise.

Choose and do one of these Challenges.

A Find out about the story of your town's coat-of-arms. (There is some information about coats-of-arms on page 150.)

B Find out how the Union Flag is made up and how to fly it. Know your country emblem and the story of its patron saint (see pages 151-152).

C Learn to communicate without speech. (There are some ideas on pages 152-153.)

D Help a new Brownie to learn her Promise, the Brownie Song or Brownie Bells.

E Find out about a historical person who was known for the good he or she did. There are some examples on pages 154-155, but you can find others. Tell your Six about this person.

...OR

think about the first part of your Promise and do your best in some other way.

When you have done your best, write about it or draw a picture of it in this box. ▼

I did my best by...

Brownies Make Things

You can use your hands, voice, arms and legs to create something which will give pleasure to others.

Choose and do one of these Challenges.

A Write a poem, short play, song or prayer and share it with a group of people.

B Create a magic show and perform it for the Pack. (There are some ideas on pages 165-167.)

C Make up a mime, dance or tune and perform it for other people.

D Use a shoe box and mirrors to make a periscope. (You can find out how on page 168.)

E Use play bricks or other materials together with paper sails to design and make a land yacht which will move when you blow it gently.

... OR

challenge yourself to be creative in some other way.

Some members of Emily's Six made puppets when they were on the Road. Emily used the puppets in the play she wrote when she was on the Highway. The whole Pack loved watching her play!

Answer these questions when you have completed your Challenge:

What did you do?

....

....

What was the most difficult part?

....

....

Were you happy with the way it turned out?

....

....

Can you say why?

....

....

....

....

There are a lot of Interest Badges connected with this Challenge. If you gain any, draw them below.

Brownies are Friendly

The Brownie Highway may not transport you to another country, but it does give you an opportunity to learn more about other people around the world.
Choose and do one of these Challenges.

A What would you like to be when you grow up? Ask your Guider if you can invite someone who does that job to come and talk to the Pack. Welcome the guest to your meeting and afterwards make a thank-you speech or write a thank-you letter. (There are some hints about inviting, welcoming and thanking guests on page 171.)

B Make a display that shows Brownie clothes from three other countries. Try to pick countries that are in three different parts of the world. Find out what these Brownies are called. Point to each country on a map. Find out something else about each country and draw its national flag. You can work by yourself or in a group.

C Draw the World Badge on paper or card and cut it up to make a jigsaw. Ask a Brownie friend to put it together again and tell her what the different parts of the badge mean (see page 170).

D Discover something about the work of a charity aid agency. (The names and addresses of some aid agencies are on page 172 to help you.) Tell your Six what you have found out. Turn out some clothes or toys which you don't need any more and take them to a charity shop.

...OR

challenge yourself in some other way to learn more about the people of the world.

Emily often visits her friend Sunita's house. One day the two girls helped Sunita's mum make curry. While the curry was cooking, Mrs Gupta talked to them about India. Then she invited Emily to stay for tea.

Wow he really, likes it!

Afterwards, Emily described what she'd learnt on this page in her Handbook. Mrs James was very interested to see what she had written. 'How about going on to do your Culture Badge?' the Guider suggested. 'I should think you could start at Level 3.'

Write down some things you discovered when doing this Challenge.

Brownies Lend a Hand

On the Brownie Highway you can make a real difference to the people and places around you.

Choose and do one of these Challenges.

A With a group of Brownies plan, organise and carry out a conservation project to improve the environment in your community. (You will need to ask an adult's permission first.)

One day Emily noticed a patch of ground covered in litter and empty bottles. After talking to Mrs James, she and her Six cleared the rubbish and took the bottles to the bottle bank. Then, with the whole Pack, they planted a tree.

B Demonstrate how to open a casualty's airway and how to lay the person in the recovery position (see pages 175-176).

C Know how to wash and clean a wound or deal with a nose bleed (see page 174). Tell your Guider what you would do and when it would be suitable for you to deal with these emergencies.

Lend a Hand in some other way.

When you have completed your Lend a Hand Challenge, write about it or draw a picture of it in this box. ▼

D Make a survey of your local area to discover how easy it would be to get around either in a wheelchair or pushing a pram. Check with your Guider before you do this.

E Collect all the junk mail that arrives in your home during one week. Use it to make something useful, for example a toy to entertain a toddler, a notebook of scrap paper, a set of playing cards suitable for snap or another game. Recycle what is left over.

My Lend a Hand Challenge

Brownies Help at Home

A Brownie on the Highway is asked to tackle some really skilful jobs in and around the house.

Choose and do one of these Challenges.

A Make and decorate a cake for a special occasion or cook a simple pudding. You can use a packet mix if you wish. See pages 188-189 for some hints on making cakes.

B Help an adult to clean a car, inside and out.

C Show an adult that you know how to operate at least three of the following appliances: electric kettle; toaster; electric mixer, whisk or food processor; cassette/CD player; video machine; oven; microwave oven; washing machine; tumble drier; dish washer. (You can find out how to use electrical appliances safely on pages 186-187.)

D Make breakfast and serve it to a special person. Remember to ask first if he or she would like breakfast!

E Show that you can clean a window or mirror so that it sparkles. Can you find a different way of cleaning a window or mirror? (There are some instructions on page 190.)

F Wash and iron the clothes you wear for Brownies and look smart at Pack meetings.

...OR

help at home in some other way.

I Help at Home

For my Challenge I . . .

. . . .

. . . .

. . . .

. . . .

Some of the Interest Badges will help you to learn more about this Challenge.

Draw and colour in any of them you gain.

Brownies Have Fun Out-of-doors

Highway Brownies learn to find their way around out-of-doors, and to observe what they see.

Choose and do one of these Challenges.

A Over a period of time watch what grows and lives on a wall. (There are some ideas on page 200.) Share what you discover with your Pack.

Emily watched the wall beside the bus stop for a few minutes every day after school. Here are her drawings of the things she saw.

B Know eight points of a compass and use a compass to find north. Use the compass to make up a treasure hunt. Make a compass of your own (see page 201).

C Identify three constellations. Make up a game to teach others in your Six about the stars. There is some information on stars and an example of an activity you could try on page 202.

D Pass a message to someone who is out of hearing range using signals or codes. (You can find out about some signals and codes on page 203.)

E Make a simple map showing the area around your meeting place or home. Give directions to the nearest shop, telephone and hospital.

F Grow something you can eat, such as a vegetable, or something you can give to someone as a present, for example flowers. (There are some hints on pages 204-205.)

Record what you did for this Challenge in the box below. ▼

··· OR

do something else that will help you to have fun out-of-doors.

Do you think that what you have just learnt will be useful when you leave Brownies for Guides? Can you say why?

My Journey Along the Brownie Highway

I started my Highway Journey

on ....

Each time you complete a Challenge write the name on a section of the Highway.

When you take part in a Pack Venture write about it on a concrete slab in the Venture Bridge.

Write down any Interest Badges you gain in this space.

One Journey Ends . . .

Like you, Emily has completed her eight Highway Challenges and has reached the end of her third Brownie Journey. She is about to replace her Brownie Road Badge with the Brownie Highway Badge.

'I've learnt so much in my three years as a Brownie,' she tells Mrs James. 'Especially about my Promise. It really makes a difference to everything I do – not just at Brownie meetings, but at home and even at school.'

Can you understand what she means? What sort of difference does your Promise make at home and at school? Perhaps you could discuss this with your Guider, and then try to note down some important things you have learnt over the last three years.

It's fun to LAH!

I enjoy a real challenge!

I have friends all over the world

...And Another Begins

By now you will have reached your tenth birthday. Are you looking for something new? Is there a Guide Unit nearby which you could visit? Perhaps you'll meet someone you knew as a Brownie.

Emily wants to find out more about Guides, so she goes to talk to Linda, her old Sixer.

The two girls go up to Linda's bedroom. Linda shows Emily the clothes she wears to Guide meetings.

'The Guide Promise is almost the same as the Brownie Promise,' she explains. 'And Guides have Laws and a Motto just like Brownies.'

'Do you like being a Guide?' Emily asks.

The question makes Linda laugh. 'I love it!' she says. She goes on to tell Emily all about her Patrol. (Patrols are a bit like Sixes.)

'There are five of us. Together we plan all sorts of exciting things to do. We work for Interest Badges, go on expeditions and cook meals outside. Sometimes we go camping, too!'

Guides sound brilliant!

Here are some things you might like to find out about Guides.

How many Guide Laws are there?

....

Which two interest you most?

1 ....

....

2 ....

....

You will need to know about your Guide Unit. Write the answers here:

Name of unit

....

Name of Guider

....

The Guides call her

....

The subscription is ....

The unit meets at

....

on ....

from .... to ....

There are ....Patrols,

called ....

....

....

....

....

127

You can find the answers to your questions by asking:

Why don't you visit a Guide Unit?

No matter how well someone describes a Guide meeting, nothing beats going to one yourself. Your Guider will arrange this for you, but it's up to you to make the most of the opportunity and find out as much as you can.

and there is more information in:

the guide handbook

The Guide Handbook tells you all about Guides and the Guide programme. In Brownies you worked for Journey Badges and met eight different kinds of Challenge. Guides work for Trefoil Badges. The eight different Challenges have more grown-up names but each still has a special symbol.

Mexican evening

The Brownie Trefoil Badge

This is the badge you will take with you from Brownies to Guides.

The Brownie Trefoil Badge is worn on your Guide badge sash. Not only does it show other people that you've been a Brownie, but it also reminds you of the fun you've had and the things you've learnt on Ventures and Journeys (things that will be very useful to you as a Guide.)

According to Emily, there's even more fun ahead.

Guides are fantastic!

Hints to Help You

The following pages contain hints on how to do some of the Challenges. You can get further ideas and help from other books suggested by your Guider or from your local library. Remember to look at your *BROWNIE* magazine, too.

Brownies are Wide Awake

Brownies Keep Healthy

Brownies Do Their Best

Brownies Make Things

Brownies are Friendly

Brownies Lend a Hand

Brownies Help at Home

Brownies Have Fun Out-of-doors

Brownies are Wide Awake

How to write your address

Miss Emily Martin
6 Pixie Row
Little Hammington
LH0 0GA.

How to use a coin telephone

1 Pick up the receiver.

2 Put in money (10p for a local call). Modern 'phones take 10p, 20p, 50p and £1 coins and have a display showing how much money is left. If this display shows that you are running out of money, put more coins in before you get cut off.

But remember that the machine doesn't give change, so for short calls don't use 50p or £1 coins.

3 Dial the number you want.

NB: Some older telephones still take only 10p coins, so remember to read the instructions carefully.

How to use a card telephone

1 Make sure you have the correct type of card for the telephone box you are using – either a British Telecom or Mercury card.

2 Pick up the receiver.

3 Put the card into the slot. The display will show you how many units are left. One unit is about 10p.

4 Dial the number.

5 When you put the 'phone down, the machine will spit out the card. Don't forget to take it!

How to pass on a message

1 Before you pick up the telephone, make sure you remember the message.

2 When the 'phone is answered, ask clearly for the person you want to talk to, using their full name.

3 When the person comes to the 'phone, check that it is the right person. Then say who you are.

4 Give them the message clearly, making sure you include important details like places and times.

May I speak to Mary Jones please?

How to contact the emergency services

You can contact the emergency services from your 'phone at home or from a public call box. You won't need any money for this.

1 Pick up the 'phone and dial 999.

2 A voice will say, 'Emergency, which service?'

3 You say clearly, 'Fire', 'Police', 'Ambulance' or 'Coastguard'.

4 The voice will repeat what you have said.

5 You should then say where you are. You may have to give the telephone number as well. This is in case you get cut off, so that help can still be sent.

6 When you are put through to the emergency service, describe the problem clearly and briefly.

How to cross the road safely

The Green Cross Code

1 First find a safe place to cross, then stop.

2 Stand on the pavement near the kerb.

3 Look all around for traffic and listen.

4 If traffic is coming, let it pass. Look all around again.

5 When there is no traffic near, walk straight across the road.

6 Keep looking and listening for traffic while you cross.

How to get help in an emergency at home

You should never use the 999 number unless it is really urgent. Here are some hints for getting help in less serious emergencies.

1 If your family has friendly neighbours, knock on their door and ask for help.

2 Keep a list of useful telephone numbers in a safe place. Include the doctor's number, and the numbers of friends and relatives living nearby. Then, in an emergency, you can ring them.

How to recycle

Do you know what these signs mean?

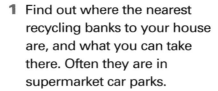

These things can easily be recycled:

1 Find out where the nearest recycling banks to your house are, and what you can take there. Often they are in supermarket car parks.

2 Before you put a can into the rubbish bin, check to see if it is made of aluminium. Often the label will tell you. Otherwise, you can test it with a magnet – an aluminium can is not magnetic, so the magnet will not stick to it. Put the aluminium can to one side to be recycled.

3 Keep empty glass bottles and jars, and sort them into different colours ready for the bottle bank. (Be very careful not to break the glass!)

4 If your local recycling centre has a plastic bank, find out what types of plastic you can take there. Look on the labels of empty plastic containers to find out what they are made of.

5 Don't throw away plastic carrier bags. Use them again next time you go shopping, or use them instead of bin-liners.

Some secret codes

Code wheel

1 Draw two circles on card with a pair of compasses. Make one circle 7 cm across and the other 8 cm across. Mark a dot in the centre of both circles.

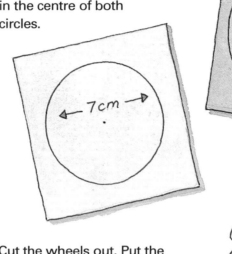

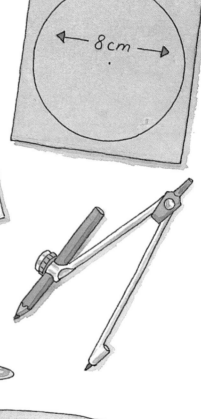

2 Cut the wheels out. Put the small one on top of the big one. Push a drawing pin through the centre dot of both wheels and into a small, hard rubber.

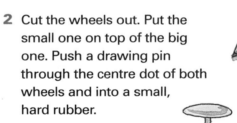

Pig-pen code

1 To make the key, first draw the patterns shown here.

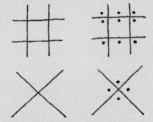

2 Now write in the letters of the alphabet like this. The pattern of lines or lines and dots next to each letter is the code for that letter.

3 This example shows what 'Brownie' looks like in pig-pen code.

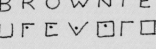

3 Draw a 6 cm wide circle in the middle of your smaller wheel.

4 Divide the rims of both your wheels into 26 spaces. Make sure the spaces on the two wheels line up.

5 Write the letters A to Z in the spaces around the rims of both wheels.

6 Now you can write your message in code. Line up one of the letters on the inside wheel (code alphabet) with A on the outside wheel (normal alphabet). Hold them together with a paper clip. Then, read off each letter in your message one by one.

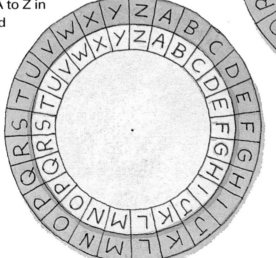

7 The person reading the code will need another code wheel like yours, and you will need to tell them how to line up the normal alphabet and the code alphabet.

The Country Code

1. Enjoy the countryside and respect its life and work.

2. Guard against all risk of fire.

3. Fasten all gates.

4. Keep your dogs under close control.

5. Keep to public paths across farmland.

6. Use gates and stiles to cross fences, hedges and walls.

7. Leave livestock, crops and machinery alone.

8. Take your litter home.

9. Help to keep all water clean.

10. Protect wildlife, plants and trees.

11. Take special care on country roads.

12. Make no unnecessary noise.

Brownies Keep Healthy

How your body works

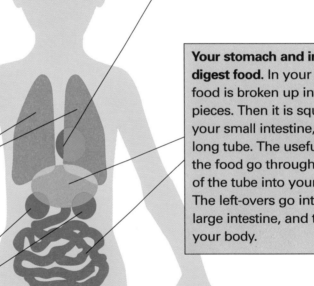

Your brain is for thinking. It also keeps your body working. Some parts of your brain think and remember things. Some parts send out messages to the rest of your body, for example to tell your arm to move. Other parts get messages from your senses.

The lungs are for breathing. In the air you breathe there is a gas called oxygen, which you need to stay alive. The oxygen goes into your blood through your lungs.

The kidneys filter your blood. They take chemicals and water that you don't need out of your blood and make urine.

The heart is a pump. It pumps blood around your body. The blood carries food and oxygen to keep you alive.

Your stomach and intestine digest food. In your stomach, food is broken up into tiny pieces. Then it is squeezed into your small intestine, which is a long tube. The useful parts of the food go through the sides of the tube into your blood. The left-overs go into your large intestine, and then out of your body.

How to care for your hair, teeth and nails

Hair

1 Brush and comb your hair at least once a day.

2 Wash your hair (or ask someone to help you wash it) once a week.

3 Use a shampoo that suits your hair type.

4 Keep your brush and comb clean.

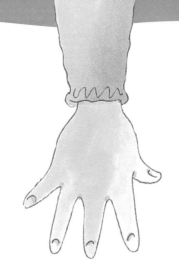

Nails

1 Keep your nails fairly short, using nail scissors or clippers.

2 Clean your nails regularly.

3 Milk contains calcium, which helps to make nails strong. Strengthen your nails by drinking some milk every day.

4 If you bite your nails, care for them by giving them the chance to grow. This is a REAL challenge!

Teeth

1 Always brush your teeth before going to bed, and after meals if possible.

2 Use a toothbrush with a small head and soft or medium bristles, and a small amount of toothpaste.

3 Brush up and down as well as from side to side. Rinse your mouth well with water.

4 Try not to eat or drink too many sugary sweets or drinks. They are bad for your teeth.

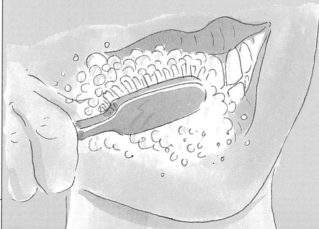

How to play sevens

The idea is to throw a ball so that it bounces against a wall and then catch it. You may think that's easy – but then you add actions. For each numbered action, you need to throw the ball and catch it that many times. If you drop the ball you have to start again from the beginning.

7 Throw the ball against the wall and catch it (seven times).

6 Throw the ball under your leg and catch it (six times).

5 Throw the ball against the wall, let it bounce on the floor once, then catch it (five times).

How to jump the blob

The blob is a bean bag fastened to a rope about three metres long. One Brownie swings the bag in a circle while another Brownie jumps over the rope.

You will need to be Wide Awake for this Challenge!

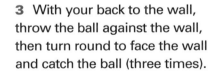

4 Throw the ball and catch it with one hand (four times).

3 With your back to the wall, throw the ball against the wall, then turn round to face the wall and catch the ball (three times).

2 Throw the ball with one hand and catch it with the other (twice).

1 Throw the ball, turn right around, clap your hands and catch the ball (once).

How to eat a healthy diet

These groups of foods are good for you:

Protein (building food)
Examples are fish, meat, cheese, nuts, beans, eggs and milk.

Carbohydrates (energy foods)
Examples are bread, potatoes, rice and pasta.

Vitamins and minerals
Examples are fruit, vegetables and liver.

For a balanced diet, you need plenty of food from all three groups.

These sorts of food aren't so good for you:

cake, biscuits, chocolate, crisps, fizzy drinks and sugar.

Don't eat too many of these.

How to stand and sit well

Your back is complicated, with lots of bones and muscles. This means that things can go wrong. If you learn to stand and sit properly, you will be less likely to get backache when you are older.

Standing

1 Put both feet flat on the floor slightly apart.

2 Hold in your bottom and stomach muscles.

3 Keep your shoulders slightly back – don't hunch them up or forwards.

4 Hold your head up.

Sitting

1 Sit straight in your chair, with your feet on the floor.

2 Rest your back against the back of the chair. Don't hunch your shoulders or curl up over a table.

How to lift heavy weights

1 Bend your knees, not your back. Keep your back straight.

2 Get a firm hold on the thing you are going to pick up.

3 If it is a heavy box, hold it underneath with both hands. If you are carrying shopping, put it in two bags and carry one in either hand to balance you.

4 Pick the object up by straightening your legs.

5 Don't carry anything that you can't pick up easily. Don't carry piles of objects – they may slip!

How drugs, solvents, alcohol and cigarettes damage your body

Drugs and solvents are chemicals that change how you think, feel and behave. People take them for different reasons. Some are just trying them out. Other people like the feelings they cause. Many want to stop but find it very difficult, because their bodies have got used to the chemicals and they feel ill without them.

Drugs

There are lots of different types of drugs. Cannabis, cocaine, amphetamines, heroin and ecstasy are a few examples, but they all have several different names. Taking any of these drugs is against the law. Using them may damage your brain and can kill you.

Solvents

Solvents are household products like glue and aerosols that give off gas or fumes. People sniff the fumes or spray them into their mouth. This can make their throat swell up so that they can't breathe.

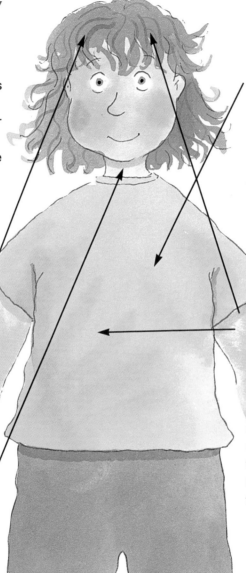

Cigarettes

Cigarettes contain a drug called nicotine. Like most drugs, it makes people feel better at first. But smoking damages your lungs, which can kill you. It is very difficult to give up smoking once you have started. It is against the law for people under 16 to buy cigarettes or other types of tobacco.

Alcohol

Alcohol is a drug which is found in drinks such as wine, beer or spirits. Small amounts of alcohol make people feel happy and relaxed. But drinking too much can make them sick or unconscious. It can also damage their liver, and may even kill them. Shops and pubs are not allowed to sell alcohol to people under 18.

How mothers and babies keep healthy

When a woman is expecting a baby, it is very important for her to eat fresh, healthy food. She is especially careful to keep food and everything in the kitchen clean. There are some foods which she avoids, such as liver, soft cheese and pâté, because they might have germs in them which could harm the baby.

A pregnant woman also takes care to keep fit. She can do gentle exercise, like swimming or yoga. She may also need to take plenty of rest. She doesn't smoke cigarettes, and probably stops drinking tea, coffee and alcohol.

A small baby needs to sleep for many hours during the day. It cannot sit, crawl, walk or talk for many months. Even so, babies like people to talk to them and to give them lots of love and attention.

As well as sleeping a lot, a baby also needs to eat very often – even at night! To start with it just drinks milk. This can be from its mother or from a bottle. At about four months old, it can start eating mashed-up food. From seven months a baby's teeth begin to appear and it can start eating more solid food.

How to play French cricket

1 One Brownie stands with her feet together holding a bat in front of her legs.

2 Everyone else makes a circle around her.

3 One Brownie throws a ball to hit the batter on the legs below the knee. Hits above the knee do not count.

4 The batter hits the ball away from her without moving her feet. She can move the bat around her legs, but mustn't move her feet.

5 If the thrower misses, whoever picks up the ball has a turn at throwing.

6 If the batter is hit below the knee, she changes places with the thrower.

How to design your own exercise routine

Do these exercises to your favourite piece of music. Choose something with a good beat!

Warming up and slowing down

Include some or all of these before and after your exercises:

1 Stand with your feet apart and bend your knees to the beat of the music (20 times).

2 March on the spot (count 20).

3 Push the heel of one foot out in front and tap your toes on the ground, then the other foot (10 times each foot).

4 Shrug one shoulder, then the other, then both together, then roll them backwards (10 times through).

5 Swing arms to the right, then the left (10 times each way).

6 Stand with feet apart. Stretch one arm over your head and put your other hand on your hip. Lean over to the side with your arm curved over your head. Then do the same on the other side.

8 Lie on your back with your legs bent and feet on the floor. Pull one knee into your chest. Then straighten the knee and carefully pull it towards you until you feel a stretch behind your knee. Only go as far as you find comfortable. Change legs.

7 Stand with one foot 30 cm behind the other, both pointing forwards. Bend the front leg slowly, keeping the back heel down, until you feel a stretch in the calf of your back leg. Change legs.

9 Stand up straight with feet apart. Bend over until your hands almost touch the floor, letting your arms hang loose. If you can touch the floor easily, rest your hands between your feet, but don't stretch. Stay there for 10 seconds, breathing deeply. Slowly straighten up, lifting your head last.

Exercises

Include some or all of these exercises, or make up some of your own:

- Jogging on the spot.

- Jumping on both feet.

- Knee lifts – lift your knee to your chest. Lift one knee 10 times, then the other. If you're fit, do a little hop at the same time.

- Kicking high and clapping under your leg (10 times each leg). ▼

- Skipping around the room.

- Twist! Keeping your feet together, twist them quickly one way, then the other, with little jumps. Swing your arms the opposite way to your feet (10 times).

- Jumping jacks – stand with your arms by your sides, then jump to make an X shape, with your legs apart and arms up. Go back to the starting position (5 times quickly). ▼

- Spotty dogs – stand with your arms by your sides, then jump with your right leg and left arm forward, left leg and right arm back. Change arms and legs. Do this with plenty of bounce ◄ (5 times)!

- Mule kicks – crouch on the floor with your legs bent up under your stomach and your hands on the ground. Push your legs out straight, then go back to the crouching position (20 times). ▼

How to cycle safely

Before you go:

1 Check that your tyres are pumped up hard.

3 Wear the right clothes. This means a special cycle helmet, light clothes and a reflective belt or jacket. Don't wear loose clothes or long scarves that might get caught in the wheels.

2 Check that your bicycle has lights that work. If it is dark or misty, remember to use them.

4 Check that your brakes work properly.

When cycling:

1 Keep well away from busy main roads.

2 If possible, ride on a cycle path.

3 If you are riding on a road, ask an adult to show you the signals that cyclists use. Know the rules of the road. If possible, take the Cycling Proficiency Test. (Your school may arrange for you to do this.)

4 Most important of all, stay wide awake! Cars, buses, people walking and other road users may do things you aren't expecting. Make sure your eyes and ears are open.

5 Don't carry things in your hands, or hanging off your handlebars. Use a proper basket or a rucsac.

Brownies Do Their Best

The National Anthem

God save our gracious Queen,
Long live our noble Queen,
God save the Queen!
Send her victorious,
Happy and glorious
Long to reign over us,
God save the Queen!

Thy choicest gifts in store
On her be pleased to pour
Long may she reign.
May she defend our laws,
And ever give us cause
To sing with heart and voice,
God save the Queen!

How to find out about your town's coat-of-arms

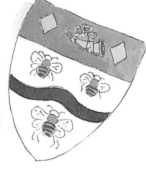

The earliest coats-of-arms were real coats worn by knights over their armour. Each coat was embroidered with a special coloured pattern which matched the pattern on the knight's shield. In battle, when a knight's face was hidden under his helmet, these patterns told everyone who he was, and so whether he was a friend or an enemy.

Today a coat-of-arms is not something you wear. It is a kind of badge with a special pattern, which tells the history of the person or place to which it belongs.

The coat-of-arms of an industrial town, for example, may show tools such as a weaver's shuttle.

The best place to find out about your town's coat-of-arms is at the public library. Ask the librarian for help. Perhaps you would like to make a sketch of the coat-of-arms and then colour it in? This drawing could be the start of a very interesting collection.

How the Union Flag is made up

This is the Union Flag, the flag you will see flying in England, Scotland, Northern Ireland and Wales. It is made up using crosses in a special way to show that these countries together form the United Kingdom. (United means joined together.)

In the background is the cross of St Andrew, the patron saint of Scotland.

Then comes the cross of St Patrick, the patron saint of Ireland.

Finally, there is the cross of St George, the patron saint of England.

The patron saint of Wales is St David, and the Welsh national flag looks like this.

There are four days each year when people particularly remember these saints.

St. David's day is March 1st. Wherever he went, he comforted and helped people. Sometimes he did this by singing to them, for he had a wonderful voice.

St. Patrick's day is March 17th. As a boy he was kidnapped and taken to Ireland as a slave. He escaped, but later returned to spend the rest of his life telling Irish people about God.

St George's day is April 23rd. Folk tales tell us that he was a soldier who always tried to obey God.

He once saved a princess very bravely, and was always ready to help other people.

St Andrew's day is November 30th. He was a fisherman and a special friend of Jesus.

The stories of the saints are interesting to read. Your local library or Guider should have a book you can borrow.

How to fly the Union Flag

As you can see in the picture, the diagonal white band is thicker on one side of the diagonal red band than on the other. When you fly the Union Flag on a flagpole, the thicker white band should be at the top on the side nearest the flagpole.

If you fly the Union Flag upside down, it's a sign that you are in trouble and that you want someone to rescue you.

How to communicate without speaking

Finger spelling

Deaf people have their own language, called sign language, so that they can talk to each other and to people who can hear.

The signs are made using both hands. Sign language has its own alphabet, with signs for each letter. It also has many signs for whole words. This is the alphabet:

Version for right-handed person

Body language

You can learn a lot about people just by watching them. How do they sit, move or walk?

Can you tell when someone is feeling tired or unhappy? The tired person may be 'droopy' and move slowly. Maybe she drags her feet or stumbles. Or perhaps you know she is tired just because she keeps yawning! An unhappy person may be quiet and withdrawn (sitting apart from others and not joining in). She may sit hunched up and turn away if you talk to her.

How do you look if you are . . .

BORED

TIRED

FRIGHTENED

HAPPY

IN PAIN

ANXIOUS

TEARFUL

INTERESTED

ANGRY

Try acting some of these and see if the others in your Six can guess what mood you are in.

If you can see what sort of mood someone is in without that person needing to tell you, you'll be very good at communication. This way of showing your moods is called body language – your body speaks for you! How do you think you look to other people?

People in history who did good

Elizabeth Fry (1780-1845)

In the past, girls and women were supposed to stay at home and know nothing about crime. But Elizabeth Fry visited prisons, where men and women were locked up in cells together without proper beds, clothes or food. She read to the prisoners and gave them clothes. She also persuaded the government and the people who ran the prisons to improve conditions.

▼ Florence Nightingale (1820-1910)

Although Florence Nightingale's parents thought that girls should not work for a living, Florence was determined to be a nurse. In 1854, when the British army was fighting the Russians in the Crimea, she went there to look after wounded soldiers. The hospital was very dirty and many soldiers were dying. Florence made sure that the wards were cleaned and that the patients had proper food. She saved the lives of many soldiers who would otherwise have died.

▲ Mohandas Gandhi (1869-1948)

India was ruled by the British government, but many Indians wanted to rule their own country. Gandhi believed that the best way to fight the British was not by violence but by peaceful protests and prayer. People listened to him because he was a very holy man – he gave up all his belongings, wore very simple clothes and ate only vegetables and fruit. He was arrested several times, but eventually his peaceful protests succeeded. In 1947 India was given its freedom.

Mother Teresa of Calcutta (born 1910)

The Roman Catholic nun, Mother Teresa, travelled to Calcutta in India and became a teacher. She was very worried about the terrible lives of the very poor people in Calcutta, so she started up new schools and hospitals for them. Her work with homeless, ill and starving people has made her famous.

▼ Harriet Tubman (1820-1913)

Harriet Tubman was born as a black slave in America. This meant that she was owned by white people, who could do what they liked to her. When she was 29 she escaped, and went to live in the north of the country where it was against the law to own slaves. Over the next 16 years she helped 300 other black people to escape. This was very dangerous. She also helped to start schools for black people.

▲ Johnny Appleseed (1774-1845)

Johnny Appleseed lived in America at a time when many people were moving there from Europe to build new farms. He travelled around the country planting apple trees and other fruit trees. When people came to build farms in those places, they found his trees waiting for them. He was also famous for being kind to animals.

Brownies Make Things

How to make a Diwali lamp

For the Diwali Festival of Light, girls in India make lamps to light in their homes. Sometimes they float them across a river when it gets dark. If the lamp is still alight at the other side, they take it as a sign that they will have some good luck in the next year.

You will need:
- self-hardening clay (powder)
- salad oil
- candle wick or a piece of cotton string.

1 Mix the clay powder with water until it is smooth. You may need an adult to help you do this.

2 Roll a ball of clay about the size of an orange. Press your thumb in the middle of the ball and shape it into a shallow bowl.

3 Pull out one side to look like the lip of a jug.

4 Leave to dry well.

5 With an adult to help you, put a little salad oil into the bowl. Put one end of a short length of candle wick or cotton string into the oil, with the other end resting on the lip.

6 You can now light the end of the wick.

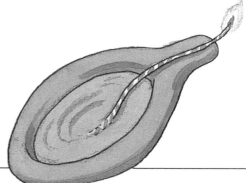

How to make a gift using natural materials

Here are some ideas you might like to try.

▼ A decoration made from a fir cone and a conker.

◄ A paperweight, made from a smooth stone, which has been cleaned, painted and varnished.

▲ A necklace made from melon seeds, dyed and threaded together.

How to make a game for a small child

Up the umbrellas, down the chimneys

You will need:

- a sheet of A 4 card (297 x 210 mm)
- felt-tipped pens, ruler and pencil
- 6 used party poppers or other counters
- 1 dice and a shaker.

1 First, draw a line across your card 4 cm from the edge. Then draw nine lines, 3 cm apart, from this line to the opposite edge, and five more lines across your card 3 $\frac{1}{2}$ cm apart. This should give you a long strip across the top and 50 squares (see below).

2 Write the title at the top.

3 Number the squares from 1 to 50. Put START on the first square and FINISH on the last square.

4 Draw on umbrellas and chimneys leading from one square to another. Make them different lengths. Colour the whole board with felt-tipped pens.

5 Play the game like snakes and ladders, but going up the umbrellas and down the chimneys. Use empty party poppers as counters. Decide on the rules before you start playing – for example, do you need to throw a six to start?

Small children love to play with puppets. You can find out how to make puppets on pages 162-164.

If you are making a toy for a very young child, it is important not to use anything sharp or to have any loose pieces which the child could put into her mouth, nose or ears. Make sure you sew or glue any small objects like beads very firmly onto the toy.

How to make something useful for Brownies

Bean bags

You will need:
- small rectangular scraps of cloth
- lentils
- a needle and thread.

1 Fold the rectangle of cloth in half widthways, with the patterned sides together.

2 Sew along two sides.

3 Turn the bag inside out and fill with lentils.

4 Turn the edges of the opening under and sew neatly.

5 To make a triangular bean bag, pull the two corners on the unsewn side together. This makes a straight edge. Turn the edges under and sew neatly.

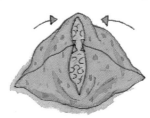

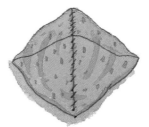

A sitter

1 Decorate the card in any way you like, for example with felt-tipped pens or by sticking on felt or paper shapes. You need to decorate both sides of the card.

2 When the card is dry, put it inside the plastic bag. Fold over the extra plastic and stick it down with tape.

fold here

3 If you wish, you can make a more complicated design. Maybe you could weave your sitter from some strips of coloured card.

A cover for your Handbook

1 Make a 1 cm hem all around the edge of the piece of material.

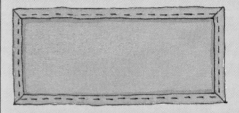

2 Fold over 4 cm at one end of the material and sew it down to make a pocket. (Perhaps an adult can help you to do this.)

3 Do the same at the other end. These pockets are for the covers of your Handbook to slot into.

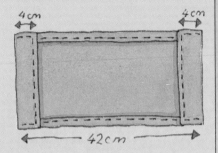

4 Turn the Handbook cover over and decorate the outside using fabric paints or crayons.

A pencil holder

You will need:

- the centre of a kitchen roll, cut to half its length
- coloured, sticky-backed plastic, or material, wallpaper or thin card
- a piece of card 6 cm x 6 cm
- glue and sticky tape.

1 Stick the kitchen roll to the small piece of card using sticky tape.

2 Cover the roll with the coloured plastic, material, wallpaper or card. Decorate it in any way you like – use your imagination!

How to make a table decoration

You will need:

- a coffee jar lid
- plaster of Paris
- a candle
- some natural objects, such as shells, cones, pebbles or dried flowers.

1 Mix the plaster of Paris with water. (You will need to read the instructions.) Pour it into the coffee jar lid.

2 Before the plaster sets, stand a candle in the middle and decorate around it with the natural objects.

3 When the plaster is dry, decorate the outside of the coffee jar lid by sticking on coloured paper or more shells.

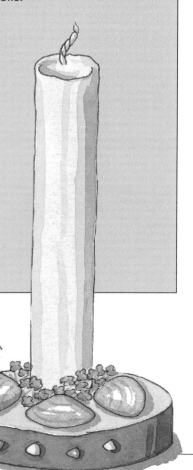

How to make puppets

Glove puppet

You will need:

- a piece of felt twice the size of your hand
- a small piece of felt for the face
- wool for hair.

1 Fold the felt in half. Put your hand in the middle of the felt, with your thumb and little finger held out to the sides. Draw round your hand to make a pattern.

fold

2 Cut two pieces of felt to this shape and glue or sew them

4

3 Cut a circle of felt for the face. Draw eyes and a mouth using felt-tipped pens, or sew them on with embroidery thread. Glue the face to the puppet's head.

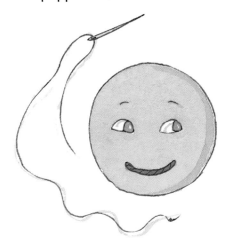

Glue

Newspaper puppet

You will need:
- newspaper
- tissue paper, crêpe paper or material.

1 Tightly roll up two or three pages from a newspaper. Do this twice to make two rolls.

2 Using sticky tape, join the two rolls together to make a cross shape.

3 Wrap tissue paper, crêpe paper or material around the arms.

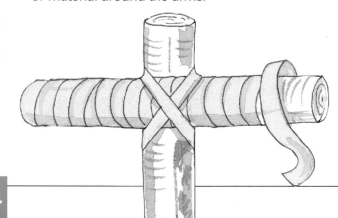

4 For the skirt, cut out a rectangle of tissue paper, crêpe paper or material. The short sides of the rectangle will need to be the same length as your puppet's 'legs'. The long sides of the rectangle should be about twice as long. Sew or glue the short sides together to make a tube. Then gather up one end of the tube and glue it around the puppet's waist.

5 Cut out a face from a magazine and stick it to the front of the puppet's head.

How to do some simple magic tricks

Make sure you have everything ready before you start a trick. Practise in front of a mirror until you know the trick really well.

Simon says

You will need:

- six used matches
- a drinking straw
- a bowl of water
- soap and sugar.

To get ready:

1 Fill one end of the straw with soap and dip the other end in damp sugar.

2 Wipe the tips clean so that nobody can see what you've done.

The trick:

1 Float six matches in a bowl of water.

2 Dip the soapy end of the straw in the water. Say 'Simon says go away.' The matches start drifting away to the edge of the bowl.

3 Take the straw out and wave it around like a magic wand. While you do this, turn it round so that the other end is pointing at the water. Don't let anyone guess what you are doing!

4 Dip the sugary end of the straw in the water. Say 'Simon says come back.' The matches float back into the middle!

The vanishing coin

You will need:

- a large piece of white paper
- a small piece of white paper
- a sheet of coloured paper
- a glass
- a coin
- glue
- a pencil.

To get ready:

1 Put the glass upside-down on the smaller piece of white paper and draw round it. Cut out the circle and glue it over the top of the glass. Cut off any bits that stick out.

2 Cut a piece of coloured paper the same height as the glass. Wrap it round the glass. Stick the edges together. This is a cover for the glass. Make sure it slips on and off the glass, but not too easily.

3 Put the large piece of white paper on a table. Put the upside-down glass, the coloured paper cover and the coin on the paper.

The trick:

1 Put the coloured paper cover over the glass.

2 Pick up the glass with the cover on it. Make sure you hold them tightly so that the glass doesn't slip out. Put them over the coin.

3 Lift off the paper cover. Hey presto, the coin has vanished!

4 Put the cover back over the glass and lift them both. The coin reappears! Put the glass in its cover back down on the white paper and lift off the cover. The glass looks quite normal as long as it's on the white paper. But don't lift it off without its cover!

Amazing Aces

You will need:
- a pack of cards
- a magic wand.

To get ready:

Put the four Aces face down on the top of the pack. Don't let anyone see you doing it, and don't shuffle the cards.

The trick:

1 Ask your friend to pick up the pack and divide it into four piles about the same size. Make sure you see where she puts the top of the pack (with the four Aces on top of it). Line the four piles up, with the pile with the Aces in it last.

2 Point to the first pile. Ask your friend to pick it up. Then ask her to move the top three cards to the bottom of the pile.

3 Ask your friend to deal one card from the top of that pile onto the top of each of the other piles. Then put the pile back where it was.

4 Repeat steps 2 and 3 with the three other piles, finishing with the pile that has the Aces in it.

5 Wave your magic wand over the four piles of cards. Then ask your friend to turn over the top card of each pile. Amazing! There are the four Aces!

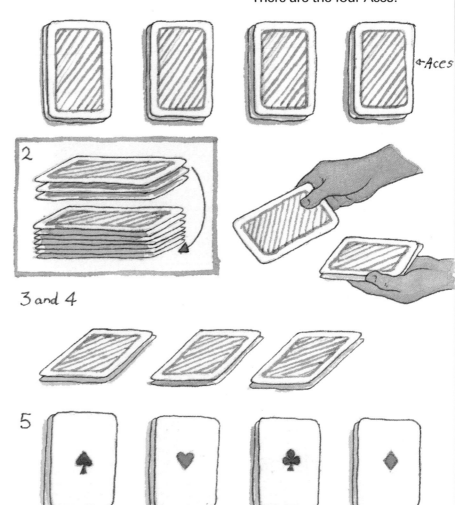

1

2

3 and 4

5

167

How to make a periscope

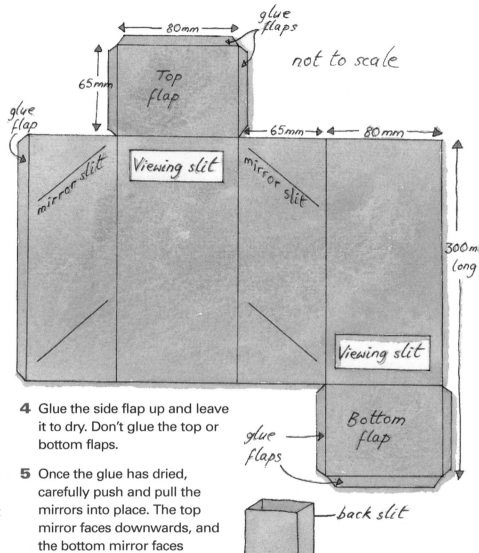

not to scale

1 Cut out the shape opposite from card. Carefully mark on all the lines and flaps, score them with the knife and fold them.

2 Cut your mirrors to 65 x 90 mm.

3 Cut out the viewing holes with the craft knife and carefully make slits for the mirrors. Don't make the slits too big – it is easy to make them bigger later on, but impossible to make them smaller! Try the mirrors in them to make sure they are just big enough.

4 Glue the side flap up and leave it to dry. Don't glue the top or bottom flaps.

5 Once the glue has dried, carefully push and pull the mirrors into place. The top mirror faces downwards, and the bottom mirror faces upwards.

6 Tuck in the top and bottom flaps, but don't glue them.

How to knit

There are many different knitting stitches, but the easiest is called garter stitch. Once you have learnt this, you can use it to knit blankets, scarves, and all sorts of toys as well. (Ask your Guider where you can find patterns for these.)

First of all, you will need to find someone to show you how to 'cast on' your stitches. After that it's up to you. Garter stitch is easy. Keep needle A in your left hand and needle B in your right. All you have to do is remember four words:

In

Push needle B into the stitch.

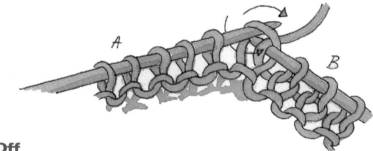

Over

Bring the wool over needle B.

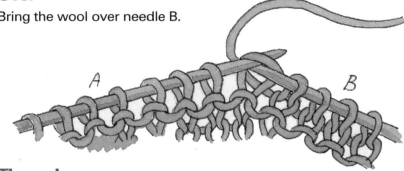

Through

Draw the wool through the stitch using needle B.

Off

Carefully slip the stitch off needle A.

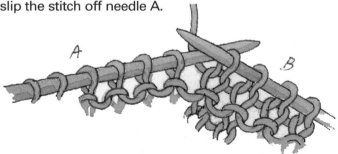

Keep knitting stitches in this way, from needle A to needle B, until you reach the end of the row. Then turn your knitting round and start the next row. NB: Make sure you have the same number of stitches in each row. Get someone to show you how to cast off.

Brownies are Friendly

How to make a friendship circle

1 Take a square piece of paper (about 14 cm x 14 cm) and fold it in half diagonally.

2 Fold the paper in half diagonally two more times.

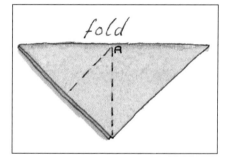

3 Place the folded paper flat with the centre point (A) nearest to you and draw the shape of a girl, as shown in this picture.

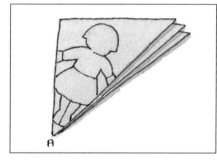

4 Cut along the dotted lines.

5 Open out the triangle and colour in the shapes to make all the members of the Guiding family in Britain.

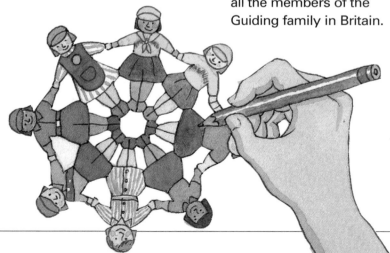

The World Badge

Guides and Brownies everywhere wear a World Badge, which looks like this.

The three leaves of the trefoil stand for the three parts of the Promise. The vein in the centre is a compass needle, pointing the way, and the two stars stand for the Promise and the Law. The 'stalk' at the bottom looks like a flame and stands for the love of all people. The colours remind us of the golden sun shining over all the people of the world from a blue sky.

How to invite and welcome a guest to your Brownie meeting

Your Pack has decided that you want to invite someone to your meeting place. Perhaps you'd like a member of the local cycling club to show you how to care for your bicycles. Or maybe you've made some toys for your local playgroup and you want to give them to its leader.

1 At least two weeks in advance, write an invitation on a piece of writing paper or a card. Even better, decorate the card yourselves. Use your best writing. Explain who you are and why you would like the person to come to your meeting. Give the date and time.

2 The week before, write again to remind your guest that you are looking forward to their visit. Draw a little map to show where your meeting place is. On the map, show where your guest can park their car, and where the nearest bus stop is, with the number of the bus.

3 On the evening, keep a look out for the visitor. If the person is carrying bags, offer to carry them to the hall. You might like to write a little welcoming speech, and a thank-you speech for the end of the visit.

4 You could make refreshments, but check beforehand with your Guider. (Remember that people from some cultures may not eat some sorts of food.)

Dear Mrs Smith
We are New Town Brownie Pack.
We have made some soft toys for your playgroup and would like you to come and receive them at NewTown Village Hall 6.P.m. 2nd August.

Charity aid agencies

All these organisations will send you leaflets or posters about their work.

World Wide Fund for Nature (WWF)

Panda House
Weyside Park
Godalming
Surrey
GU7 1XR
Tel: 0483 426444
(nature and the environment)

Oxfam

274 Banbury Road
Oxford
OX2 7DZ
Tel: 0865 311311
(helping people in poor countries)

Save the Children Fund

Mary Datchelor House
17 Grove Lane
London
SE5 8SP
Tel: 071 703 5400
(caring for children in the UK and abroad)

Age Concern (England)

Astral House
1268 London Road
London
SW16 4EJ
Tel: 081 679 8000
(caring for old people)

Age Concern also has offices in Scotland, Wales and Ulster. These are the telephone numbers. Ask your Guider to 'phone for the address.

Scotland: 031 228 5656
Ulster: 0232 245729
Wales: 0222 371566

International Red Cross/Red Crescent

British Red Cross Society
9 Grosvenor Crescent
London SW1X 7EJ
Tel: 071 235 5454
(emergency aid in this country and abroad)

Brownies Lend a Hand

How to treat simple burns and scalds

1 Cool the affected part by putting it in cold water or under a gently running tap.

2 Keep it in cold water until it stops hurting.

3 Do not prick or break blisters.

4 Do not put lotions, antiseptics or anything greasy on the burn.

5 Wash your hands well. Put a light, clean covering, such as a clean handkerchief or clean plastic bag, over the burn. Do not use sticking plaster or anything fluffy or hairy.

How to deal with clothes on fire

1 Do not let the person run outside.

2 Wrap a coat or rug around the person, calling for help at the same time.

3 Push her to the ground.

4 Smother the flames with the coat or rug.

5 Make her comfortable.

6 Fetch an adult immediately.

If you don't have anything to wrap around the burning clothes, make the person stand still, push her onto the ground and roll her over and over.

How to wash and clean a simple wound

1 Wash your hands and dry them on a clean towel.

2 Clean the wound under running water and wipe from the centre outwards using clean material.

3 Keep the wound clean by covering it with a sticking plaster or a piece of gauze held in position with bandage.

4 If there is glass in the wound, do not take it out. Take the patient to hospital.

How to treat a nose bleed

1 Tell the patient to sit with her head tipped forward.

2 Firmly pinch the soft part of her nose for ten minutes. Ask her to breathe through her mouth. If her nose has not stopped bleeding after ten minutes, keep pinching it for another ten minutes.

3 Do not let the patient blow her nose, but give her a cloth or tissue to mop up the blood.

4 Tell an adult what has happened.

If you have any open cuts or grazes on your hands, it is important not to let someone else's blood get into them. Make sure you cover them with a sticking plaster before treating someone who is bleeding. If you have a first aid kit with plastic gloves in it, wear them to treat the patient.

How to open a blocked airway

If someone is unconscious, her airway may be blocked, making it difficult for her to breathe. This is because the tongue blocks the throat.

1 If there is anything in the mouth, take it out with your fingers.

2 With your fingers under the patient's chin, put your other hand on her forehead and tilt her head well back.

How to put someone in the recovery position

If someone is unconscious, after you have opened the airway, you should put her in the recovery position.

1 If she is lying on her back, gently straighten her arms and legs. Kneel on her right-hand side.

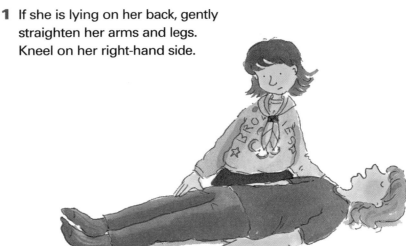

2 Put her right arm out to one side, bent upwards at the elbow, with the hand pointing upwards and the palm up.

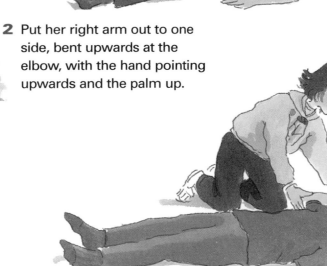

3 Bring her left arm across her chest. Put the hand next to the patient's right cheek, with the palm outwards. Hold it there with your left hand.

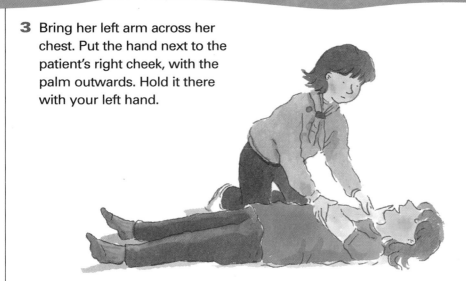

4 With your right hand, get hold of her left thigh and lift her knee. Pull at the thigh to roll her towards you onto her side. Keep her left hand pressed against her cheek.

5 Tilt her head back to make sure the airway stays open. Her left hand should keep her head in this position.

6 Make sure her left (top) leg is bent well up at the knee.

7 Once you have put the patient in the recovery position, it is safe to leave her alone while you call an ambulance.

If the patient has injured her arms, legs or back, you must be especially careful when turning her over. Use rolled-up blankets or clothes to hold her on her side if you can't bend her arms or legs.

How to use scissors and knives safely

1 When using scissors and knives, keep sharp edges well away from your fingers. Always cut away from you, not towards you.

2 To carry a pair of scissors, hold the blades. Hold a knife by the handle with the blade pointing towards the floor.

3 To pass a pair of scissors or a knife, hold the blades very carefully and let the other person take hold of the handle.

How to use tools safely

Sandpaper

You can buy very rough sandpaper, for smoothing very rough surfaces, and smooth sandpaper for smooth surfaces. It is best to wrap a piece of sandpaper around a block of wood to give you something to grip.

Screwdriver

Use a screwdriver which matches the size of your screw. Keep your hand well away from the sharp end, in case it slips.

Pliers

Use them to grip something firmly, well away from your body.

Saw

To cut wood, you will need a sharp saw. Press down fairly firmly with the saw blade, keeping your wrist strong. Hold the wood steady with your other hand, keeping it well away from the saw. Move the saw backwards and forwards slowly, with long stroking movements.

Paintbrush

Use the right size of paintbrush: for painting small things, use a paintbrush no more than half the width of the thing you are painting. Dip your brush in the paint and get rid of any drips. Paint smoothly, covering the surface well but avoiding dribbles. Afterwards, clean the brush using water or white spirit (check on the paint pot which you should use).

Hammer

If you are hammering a nail in, hold it steady at the bottom with the thumb and first finger of one hand. Give a few very gentle taps with the hammer until the point of the nail is stuck in the wood. Then take your thumb and finger away before you hammer the nail right in. Make sure you hit it straight and not too hard.

How to care for a bicycle

1 Check that your tyres are properly pumped up. Press down very hard on the tyre with your thumb. If the tyre squashes at all, it is too soft.

4 Check that your lights are working properly. Replace the batteries when the light starts to get dim.

2 If your bicycle gets wet or muddy, you should wash it. Use a bucket of warm soapy water and an old brush. Dry your bike with an old rag, especially any shiny metal parts.

3 Oil all the moving parts. This means the pedals, the parts where the pedals turn, the brakes and the chain. Use a small oil can with a dropper or spray.

5 Check for signs of wear and tear on tyres, brakes and cables. Make sure the chain isn't rusty or loose, that the wheels turn freely and that no spokes are loose.

How to tie knots

Reef knot

Although the reef knot can be used to join two ropes of the same thickness, it really only holds strongly enough to join the two ends of one piece of rope. It is used for bandages because it lies flat and is easy to untie.

1 Hold one end in your right hand and the other in your left hand.

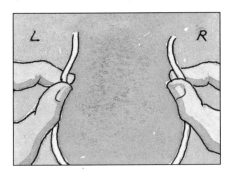

2 Lay the right over the left, tuck it under and up.

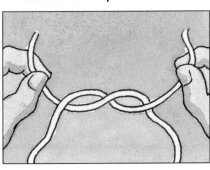

3 Lay the left over the right, tuck it under and up.

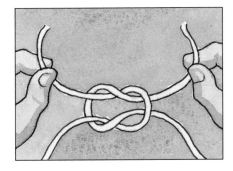

4 Pull both ends firmly away from each other.

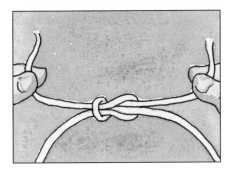

Pedigree cow hitch

This knot is useful for tying one end of a rope onto a post (for example to tie up a dog). It is not strong enough to hold a lot of weight.

1 Double over a short length at the end of the rope.

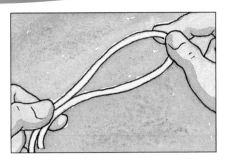

2 Fold over the doubled end to make two loops.

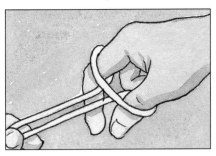

3 Slip both loops onto a post.

4 Tuck one of the ends through the opposite way.

Brownies Help at Home

How to hand wash small items of clothing

1 Use hand-hot water with just enough soap powder or liquid to make a slight lather. Check that you are using a powder or liquid suitable for hand washing, not automatic machines.

2 Turn the item inside out to wash it. Rub it gently in the water.

3 Rinse well to get all the soap out.

4 Rinse again with a fabric softener (if you use one).

5 Hang the items out to dry.

How to hang out clothes

1 Gently shake the item of clothing so that it hangs straight.

2 Hang the item up by an opening – the bottom of a T-shirt, the top of a pair of trousers or a skirt. Use at least two pegs on one edge of the opening, and let the other hang freely. This lets the air flow through it, so that it dries more quickly.

How to do simple ironing

1 Iron clothes when they are still quite damp.

2 Check on the label of each item of clothing whether it needs a cool, warm or hot iron. Sometimes this is shown by symbols.

3 Smooth any creases out of the item of clothing with your hands before starting to iron. Don't leave the iron sitting on the material or it will burn it. And take care not to burn yourself!

Pegs

How to pack a suitcase or a travel bag

Before beginning to pack, it is a good idea to make a list of the things you will need. (You don't want to miss your first pyjama party because you've forgotten your pyjamas!)

This is a well packed suitcase:

1 Heavy things like books and shoes go at the bottom. The soles of the shoes should go against the sides of the case.

2 Then come underclothes, pyjamas and towels.

3 Above that go jeans, sweaters and things that don't crease easily.

4 At the very top are skirts and T-shirts.

5 Knobbly things, such as your wash-bag, fit in around the sides.

6 Socks can be squeezed into the corners.

As you can see, the clothes have been folded into rectangles. This means that they fit neatly into the case.

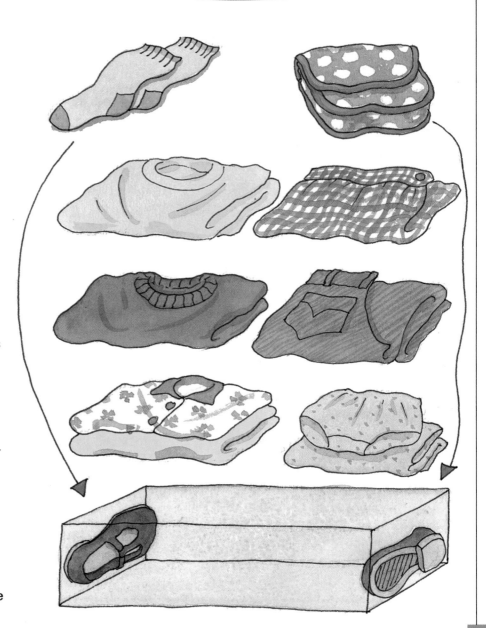

◄ How to lay a table

This is a place set for a special meal.

The knife is on the right and the fork is on the left. The soup spoon is outside the knife, and the dessert spoon goes above the place mat, with the dessert fork underneath.

There's also a glass on the right, a side plate on the left and a napkin on top of the side plate.

What else might you need on the table besides cutlery and crockery?

How to clean muddy shoes

1 Cover the table or floor with newspaper and wear an apron.

2 Remove the mud from the shoes. (It will come off easily if you let it dry.)

3 Choose a polish that matches the colour of the shoes.

4 Look at the shoe brushes. Usually there are two sorts – one for polishing and one for shining. You will know which is which because a brush for shining is much cleaner than a polishing brush.

5 Using the polishing brush, carefully cover the toes, heels and sides of the shoes with polish. Leave it for a few minutes.

6 Now take the shining brush (or wrap the polishing brush in a duster or rag) and rub the shoes until they shine.

How to clean a bath

1 Some types of bath can get scratched quite easily, so choose a cream cleaner and a soft cloth.

2 Pour a little cream cleaner around the bath and leave it for five minutes. This lets it work on any grease.

3 Scrub hard. Don't forget to wipe the taps.

4 Rinse your cloth out and wipe the cream cleaner off. It helps if you run the water at the same time, to wash away any bubbles.

5 Wipe the bath dry.

NB: You can clean a wash-basin or shower in the same way.

How to sew on a button

1 Thread your needle with a double length of thread.

2 Decide where you are going to put the button. Attach the thread to that spot, either with a knot or by making a small stitch and going over it twice.

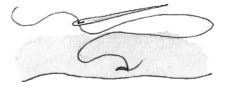

3 Slide the button down the thread.

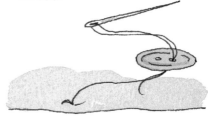

4 Sew the button on by working the needle down through one hole and up through another.

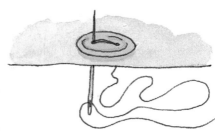

5 When the button is firmly in place, wind the thread tightly several times around its base. Finish off by pushing the needle through the 'stalk' you have made.

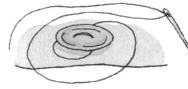

How to sew on a badge

1 Thread your needle, using thread that matches the colour of your badge.

2 Decide where you are going to put the badge and pin or safety pin it into place.

3 Make three small stitches in the same place close to the edge of the badge.

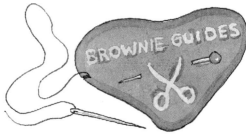

4 Work along the edge, sewing with evenly spaced diagonal stitches.

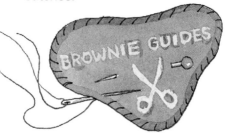

5 Finish your work firmly with three diagonal stitches in the same place.

Use the same method to sew on a patch or name tape.

How to make up a bed

1 Strip the bed completely. Put the dirty sheets and pillowcases in the wash basket or washing machine.

2 Put back the underblanket, if you have one, and the bottom sheet. Tuck in the wide hem of the sheet at the top of the bed. Smooth out wrinkles, then tuck the sides in neatly.

3 Shake your pillow. Put a clean pillowcase on, tucking it in neatly, and put the pillow back at the top of the bed.

4 If you have sheets and blankets, put them back on one at a time, tucking them in one by one. Remember to leave about 30 cm of sheet to spare at the top for turning down over the blankets.

5 If you have a duvet, shake it and put a clean cover on it. An easy way to do this is to start with the clean cover inside out, then put your hands into the top corners, grip the top corners of the duvet and pull it through. Put it neatly on the bed.

185

How to make tea

1 Empty out any water that is in the kettle and fill it up with fresh water from the tap. Boil it.

2 Warm the teapot with a little boiled water.

3 To make tea for four people, put three teaspoons full of tea or three tea-bags into the pot. (For two people use two teaspoons of tea or two tea-bags.)

4 Take the teapot to the kettle and pour boiling water onto the tea.

5 Let the tea stand for about three minutes before pouring it.

6 If you are using tea-leaves instead of tea-bags, use a tea-strainer as you pour the tea.

How to make coffee

1 Put one teaspoon of instant coffee per person into a warmed coffee-pot or jug.

2 Pour on boiling water – about one mugful per person.

3 Stir well.

4 Serve immediately with warm or cold milk.

How to use electrical appliances safely

Wires

● Do not use worn or damaged flexes (wires). Don't let pets chew electric flexes – this is very dangerous for them and for you!

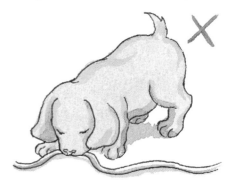

● Do not let flexes hang down where children could grab them.

● Do not let flexes touch hot parts of heaters or cookers.

Sockets and switches

- If possible, don't use adaptors – one socket, one plug.

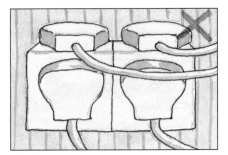

- Never poke anything into the holes of an electric socket.

- Never touch plugs, switches or electrical appliances with wet hands. Don't use appliances in the bathroom.

- Switch off and unplug all appliances before you clean them.

- Never pull out a plug by the flex.

- Turn off the appliance and the wall switch before unplugging.

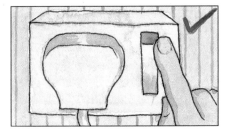

Electric fires

- Fix a fireguard in front of the fire.

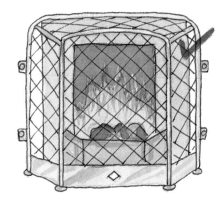

- Keep the fire well away from furniture, curtains or doors.

- Never hang clothes to dry over an electric fire or heater.

Kettle

Switch off the kettle and take the flex out before you fill or pour it. Fill it with enough water to cover the heating element.

Toaster

If bread gets stuck inside, switch off the toaster and unplug it before trying to get the bread out. Don't use a knife or other metal object.

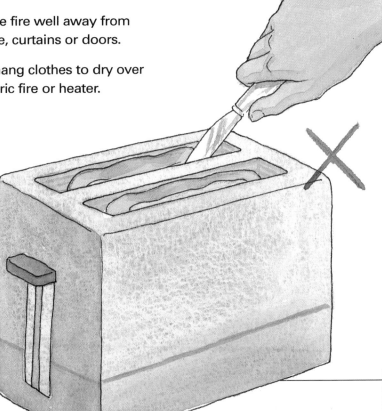

How to make a cake

Some general hints on baking:

1 Put on an apron and wash your hands before you begin.

2 Turn on the oven at the start, so that it is at the right temperature by the time you want to cook.

3 Read the recipe carefully and check you have all the ingredients.

4 If you are using a cake tin, grease it well or your cake will stick.

5 Measure your ingredients carefully using scales or standard measuring spoons.

6 Keep an eye on the clock while your cake is in the oven, but don't open the oven door too soon or it will go flat.

7 Always clear away and wash up when you have finished.

Sponge cake

You will need:

- 250g (8oz) butter or margarine
- 250g (8oz) castor sugar
- 4 eggs
- 250g (8oz) self-raising flour.

1 Turn the oven to 180°C (350°F), Gas Mark 4.

2 Grease the inside of two 20 cm (8 inch) cake tins and line the inside with grease-proof paper.

3 Beat together the butter and sugar in a bowl using a wooden spoon or an electric mixer until the mixture is a pale colour.

4 Beat the eggs, then add them to the mixture a little at a time. Beat the mixture well each time you put in some of the eggs.

5 Gently stir in the flour.

6 Pour the mixture into the cake tins and bake for 25 to 30 minutes.

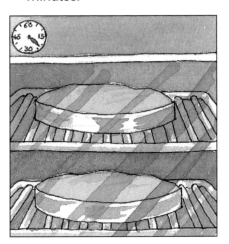

7 Sandwich them together with your favourite flavour of jam (strawberry or apricot works well).

For the icing

You will need:
- 125g (4oz) icing sugar
- 50g (2oz) butter.

Sieve the icing sugar. Beat in the butter until the mixture is smooth. Spread it over the top of the cake and sprinkle 'hundreds and thousands' or coloured sweets on top.

How to clean windows

1 Put a small amount of warm water and a tiny bit of washing-up liquid into a bucket.

2 Wet a shammy-leather in the water and squeeze it out. Clean the windows carefully, rinsing the leather every now and then.

3 Use an old toothbrush to clean into the corners of the frames.

4 Rinse the leather in clean water, squeeze it out and wipe the windows over again.

5 For a real sparkle, wipe the windows with a clean, dry cloth (not a fluffy one).

An old-fashioned method

1 Scrumple up old newspapers.

2 Sprinkle on a few drops of vinegar.

3 Polish the windows until all the streaks have gone.

Brownies Have Fun Out-of-doors

What to look for under a stone or log

Snails and slugs

Snails and slugs usually only come out at night, when it is cold and damp and there is less danger of being eaten by birds. Both snails and slugs move along on one foot, leaving a trail of slime as they go. Snails and slugs have two sets of 'feelers', one to see with (they can tell the difference between light and dark) and one to smell their food.

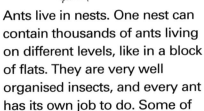

Ants

Ants live in nests. One nest can contain thousands of ants living on different levels, like in a block of flats. They are very well organised insects, and every ant has its own job to do. Some of them stay in the nest, looking after young ants. Others go outside to look for food. They can carry pieces of food almost as big as themselves.

Wood-lice

Most wood-lice only come out at night. They like dark places and they eat fallen leaves and rotting wood. They have hard armour-plating, and they can curl up into a hard ball if something attacks them.

Centipedes and millipedes

These have bodies with many hard sections, and lots of legs! They usually eat dead leaves.

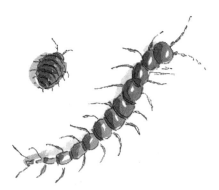

Spiders ▶

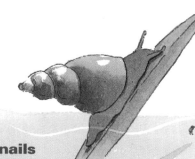

How to go pond dipping

You can make a net by bending a piece of wire 60 cm long into a circle and pushing the ends up a garden cane. Then tape up the join. Cut off one leg of a pair of tights about half-way up, and sew the open end over the wire loop. Take a large plastic tub to put your creatures in, and fill it with pond water.

A spider makes its web from strings of fine, very strong silk produced inside its body. First it lets a string float until it hits a leaf or twig. It then joins this thread to other leaves and twigs to make a 'frame'. It fills this frame with a spiral of sticky thread. When the web is finished, the spider sits and waits in the middle or at one side. Any sudden twitching tells it a small insect has been caught in the sticky threads. In other words, lunch has arrived!

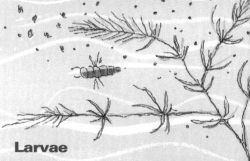

Daphnia

These are very small creatures. They swim by moving their feelers in the water.

Snails

Snails eat dead plants and animals and slime growing in the water. They sometimes move hanging down from the surface of the water, but they also move along the bottom.

Larvae

These are young insects, which hatch from eggs in the water. When they are older they turn into adults with wings and live outside the water. Larvae can look like little worms or like insects. Mosquitoes, midges, mayflies and dragon-flies all have larvae which live in water.

Water boatmen

They use their legs like the oars of a boat as they float around on the surface of the water. Some eat plants and some eat smaller animals.

What to look for in a rock pool

Starfish

Starfish are rough and spiny. On their underneath side they have hundreds of suckers which they use as feet. These suckers are also important for feeding. The starfish uses them to grab hold of small animals, and even to open shells in search of food.
◀

◀ Seaweed

Seaweeds are common seaside plants. They don't have proper roots, but cling onto the rocks or the sand with suckers.

Sea anemones ▶

A red, jelly-like blob is a closed anemone. This is an animal, but it looks a bit like a plant. It has waving tentacles and it uses these to sting small animals which it then eats. Be careful, as anemones can sting you, too.

▲ Limpets

Like many creatures that live in shells, limpets are molluscs. They cling very tightly to rocks, only moving around at high tide, when they are covered with water, to feed on nearby plants. Limpets have almost 2 000 teeth!

Water safety

We can all have lots of fun playing in or near water. Pond dipping, floating boats, making rafts, feeding the ducks or swimming are all fun as long as no one gets hurt.

Remember that the edges of ponds and rivers can be very slippery. If you fall in it can be very difficult to get out, even if you are a good swimmer. You can't usually see the bottom, and you could cut yourself on stones or broken glass. Sometimes the water has germs in it that can make you very ill.

Even at home and in the garden there are places where people can drown if they are not careful. Can you think of any? (Small children and old people are most at risk.) Maybe your Six could think of ways such accidents could happen and act them out. Then ask the other Sixes to suggest ways in which they could have stopped the accident happening.

Why not take your Water Rescuer Badge? (You do not need to be able to swim to do this.) You would learn how to keep yourself safe and how to help someone else who was in danger. Ask your Guider if the whole Pack could do this badge at your meeting place.

How to make a rain gauge

To make a rain gauge you will need a large plastic lemonade bottle with a flat bottom and a ruler.

1 Ask an adult to cut around the plastic bottle about 4 cm from the top.

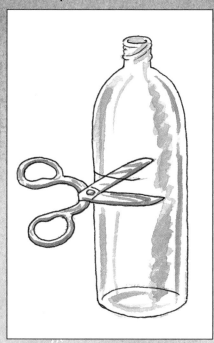

2 Put the top part of the bottle upside-down into the bottom part. This makes a funnel to collect the rain.

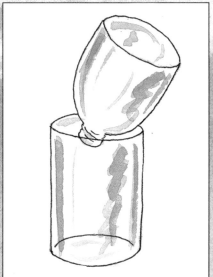

3 Sink the bottle a little way into the ground, away from trees and buildings.

4 Use a ruler to measure the amount of rain which falls in a day, or in a week.

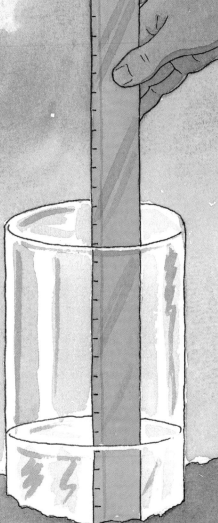

How to make a wind vane

A wind vane shows the direction in which the wind is blowing.

1 Draw the wind vane on a piece of cardboard and cut it out.

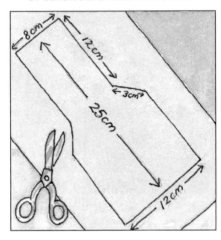

2 Cover one side with clear sticky-backed plastic.

3 Fold the wind vane in half lengthways with the plastic outwards. Cut the narrow end to make a pointer.

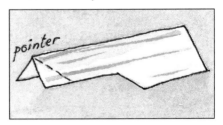

4 Using strong sticky tape, stick a pen lid half-way along the wind vane.

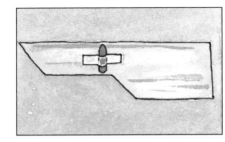

5 Ask an adult to attach a thin dowelling rod or garden cane firmly to a post or fence using electric cable clips. Sit the pen top on the wind vane over the top of the rod.

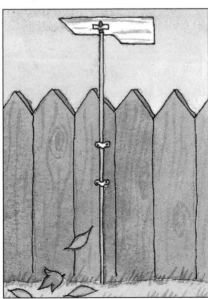

6 Using a compass, find out where north is and find a landmark to help you remember it. From that you can work out where south, east and west are. The pointer on the wind vane will point towards the direction from which the wind is blowing. So if it points towards the west, the wind is blowing from the west. This is called a west wind.

How to make a weather chart

Day	Rain in mm	Wind direction	General weather
Monday			
Tuesday			
Wednesday			
Thursday			
Friday			
Saturday			
Sunday			

At the end of the week you can add up all the rainfall for that week. Perhaps you could keep your weather chart for several weeks and compare the results.

How to go for a ramble

A ramble is a walk with a special purpose. You might visit a castle or a church. You might walk around a nature reserve. Maybe you could take a picnic. While you are on Pack Holiday, you could have a real adventure, visiting somewhere completely new.

Try to find the place you are going to on a map. What will you spot on the way? There might be a stream to paddle in on the way home!

Perhaps you could walk to the top of a hill. How far can you see? Are there any special features you can spot?

If you decide to walk through a wooded area you could look out for signs of foxes or rabbits (holes, fur and droppings, for example). You might see deer footprints, birds' nests or wild flowers. If you are quiet you will probably hear birds singing.

You can go on a ramble with your parents and friends, on school trips, or perhaps with your whole Brownie Pack.

What clothes to wear

Here is a list of suggestions:

- trainers, wellingtons or comfortable strong shoes

- comfortable sweat pants or trousers (not jeans, as these can get very heavy and uncomfortable if it rains)

- a shirt (with a collar and short sleeves if it is sunny)

- a cagoule – this is very important as you never know what the weather will do

- a sweatshirt or jumper in case it gets cold.

What to carry with you

In a rucsac put:

- an extra layer of clothing

- a map

- a camera, or notebook and pencil to draw what you see

- your lunch. (Don't take too much, as you will have to carry it! Remember not to take chocolate if it's a hot day. It's best to carry drink in a plastic bottle with a screw top, so that you can drink a little at a time.)

Have fun! Why not take Level 1 of the Walking Badge?

How to do a wall watch

1 Choose a section of wall. It needn't be very big – 90 cm wide and about 120 cm high is plenty. Mark your section of wall in a way that won't disturb it, for example by putting two stones on top of the wall, one on each side of your section.

90 cm

2 Look at your section of wall very carefully. What is it made of? Does it have a smooth surface, or are there nooks and crannies? Does the sun shine onto it or is it in the shade? What is at the bottom of the wall: grass, flower bed, pavement? Is the air clean or polluted (for example by a road nearby)?

3 Is there anything growing on the wall? Look for moss, lichen, grass, wild flowers or perhaps plants that people have planted there to make the wall look pretty. Draw pictures of the plants and try to find them in a plant book.

4 Try to watch the wall for animals and insects for about ten minutes every day. See if you can spot any harvestmen, earwigs, ants, spiders, ladybirds, caterpillars or butterflies. You could use a magnifying glass to look at them more closely.

If you keep very still and quiet you might also see birds, squirrels or cats.

5 Keep a record of the animals you see, along with the date and time and what they were doing. Draw pictures of them so that you can look them up in a book later.

How to set a compass

Imagine you are on a ramble in the countryside. To reach the nearest village you must walk in a south-easterly direction. How can you tell in what direction that is? If you have a compass in your rucsac, you can get your bearings very easily.

1 Put the compass on a flat surface.

2 Wait until the needle settles and is pointing in one direction. That direction is north.

3 Carefully turn the rim of the compass, without disturbing the needle, until the N (north) marking is under the needle. The compass is now set.

4 It is now easy to work out where the south-east is.

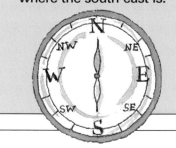

How to make your own compass

You will need:
- a small plastic container
- a needle
- a cork
- a magnet
- a sharp knife
- permanent marker pens.

1 Ask an adult to help you cut a slice of cork about 5 mm thick.

2 Magnetise the needle by stroking it several times along the magnet from eye to point in the same direction.

3 Push the needle carefully through the cork across the circle.

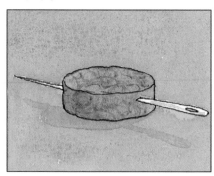

4 Fill a plastic container with water and float the cork in it. Check with a compass which end of the needle points to north and mark it on the cork. Fill in the other compass points on the cork, using a permanent marker pen.

How to spot constellations

The Plough

This is a group of seven bright stars, rather like a saucepan with a long handle. It is part of the constellation called the Great Bear. The two end stars of the Plough are called the Pointers because a line through them points to Polaris, the North Star, the only star that stands almost still in the sky. You can see the Plough at almost any time of the year.

Cassiopeia

Find the star where the Plough's 'handle' joins the 'pan', and imagine a line from there to Polaris. Then imagine the line going on beyond Polaris, and you come to a group of five stars in the shape of a W or an M. These are the constellation of Cassiopeia, a legendary queen.

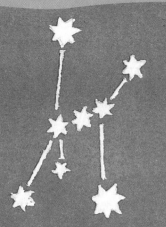

Orion

In the evening in winter, you can see the constellation Orion, the Hunter, in the south of the sky. Betelgeuse, one of the stars in Orion, is a gigantic red star called a supergiant. The three stars close together in the middle of Orion are called Orion's belt. If you draw an imaginary line through them and keep going downwards, you should find Sirius, the dog star, which is the brightest star in the sky.

The Milky Way

High in the sky in the middle of summer, on a clear night, you can see a silvery band of light stretching right across the sky. The faint light comes from hundreds of thousands of stars which are so closely crowded together that you cannot make them out. These stars form the Milky Way.

How to make a constellation game

1 Take the lid of an empty coffee jar. Inside it there should be a paper disc. Punch small holes in it in the shape of a constellation. You can find the shapes of constellations in books about stars.

2 Put silver balls (the sort that are used to decorate cakes) into the lid. Use the same number as the number of holes you have made for stars. Make sure that they are bigger than the holes!

How to signal a message

Morse code

Morse code was invented for sending messages along telegraph wires. It is made up of short and long sounds. Every letter has its own pattern of sounds. Morse code can also be written down using dots and dashes, or if it is dark you can send a message in Morse code using short and long flashes of a torch.

A .-	B -...	C -.-.
D -..	E .	F ..-.
G --.	H	I ..
J .---	K -.-	L .-..
M --	N -.	O ---
P .--.	Q --.-	R .-.
S ...	T -	U ..-
V ...-	W .--	X -..-
Y -.--	Z --..	

3 Cover the lid with cling film to keep the balls inside.

4 For the game, try to roll the balls into the holes. Can you get all the balls resting in the holes at the same time?

Semaphore

Semaphore is useful if you can see someone clearly but are too far away to shout. It's best if you use two colourful flags, but arms will do.

1 Keep your body straight and your feet slightly apart.

2 Never move from one letter until you're sure of the position of the next.

3 Bring your arms down in front of you at the end of each word.

4 Signal slowly and evenly.

5 If you make a mistake, signal E eight times.

How to grow things to eat

Tomatoes

1 You can buy tomato plants quite cheaply, or get them from other gardeners. Four plants should give your family plenty of tomatoes.

2 Around the end of May, plant your tomato plants in 20 cm pots of compost or spaced 60 cm apart in a fertilised garden bed. Put them in a sunny spot. Use sticks or garden canes to keep the plants upright as they grow.

3 Pinch off any side shoots that appear where each branch joins the main stem. Nip out the growing point when about four or five clusters of flowers have formed. Water the plant well every day.

4 After tiny green tomatoes appear, give the plants fertiliser or liquid tomato food every two weeks.

5 The tomatoes should ripen after eight to ten weeks.

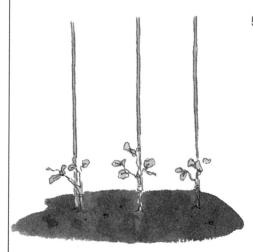

Lettuces

1 In February or March, plant a few seeds in a pot or plastic tray full of compost. Sprinkle the seeds thinly and evenly and cover them with a thin layer of compost. Wrap the pot loosely in a clear plastic bag and put it in a warm place indoors.

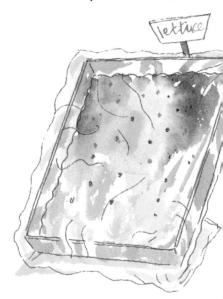

2 Water the seeds gently when the soil is dry. After five to ten days the seeds will grow into little plants, and you can take the plastic bag off.

3 Keep your pot or tray out of direct sunlight. Water the seedlings carefully when the soil is dry. If the seedlings are crowded together, snip some of them close to the ground with scissors so that each plant has plenty of room.

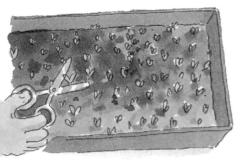

4 When the plants have two pairs of leaves, it's time to transplant them. Plant each

one in a yogurt pot full of compost to start with. Get them used to being outside by leaving them out during the daytime. When they are a bit bigger, plant them in 15 cm pots of compost or in a fertilised garden bed. Put them in a sunny spot.

5 You may need to water your lettuces once a day if it's hot. The soil should be moist but not swampy! It will be about eight weeks before you can eat them.

NB: If you sow a few seeds at a time, so that you have plants at different stages, you will get lettuces over a few weeks rather than lots all at once!

Herbs

You can grow herbs, such as parsley, mint or chives, in pots indoors on a sunny window-sill or outside in pots or garden beds. Let the pots go almost dry between waterings. Snip off leaves and shoots for cooking early in the day, when the flavour is best.

You can dry herbs in a warm, dry place (not in the sun), then store them in a jar in a dark cupboard. Try growing lavender and picking the flowers to make lavender bags.

INDEX